love, bourbon street

love, bourbon street

reflections of new orleans

edited by Greg Herren
and Paul J. Willis

 alyson books
NEW YORK

Manufactured in the United States of States.

Published by Alyson Books, P.O. Box 1253, Old Chelsea Station, New York, New York, 10115-1251.
Distribution in the United Kingdom by Turnaround Publisher Services Ltd.,
Unit 3, Olympia Trading Estate, Coburg Road, Wood Green, London N22 6TZ England.

First Edition: September 2006

06 07 08 09 a 10 9 8 7 6 5 4 3 2 1

ISBN-10 1-55583-981-9
ISBN-13 978-1-55583-981-9
The Library of Congress Cataloging-in-Publication data is available.

Book design by Victor Mingovits

*"No matter where I might roam,
New Orleans will always be my spiritual home."*

—TENNESSEE WILLIAMS

table of contents

dedication

This book is dedicated to everyone at WWL and the New Orleans *Times-Picayune*, in recognition of the outstanding work they did during Hurricane Katrina and her awful aftermath. They were a lifeline for all of us. Thank you from the bottom of our hearts. You gave us hope in the midst of horror.

May God bless you all.

acknowledgments

THIS BOOK WOULD NOT HAVE been possible without Joe Pittman, editor extraordinaire at Alyson Books, who has been patient, kind, and caring beyond belief. Thanks, Joe. You are a dream editor.

We could not even begin to list all the people, from New Orleans and all over the country, whose kindness, love, and concern made those awful months so much easier to deal with for the two of us. We thank you all. But some went above and beyond the call of duty, and they bear mentioning.

Our families took us in, gave us food, shelter, and love. We love you all.

Greg Wharton and Ian Philips have always been there for both of us, whenever we needed them, no matter the time, day, or place. You boys are angels.

Patricia Brady has also been an angel of love for the two of us, and has made our lives richer just by being our friend.

Bev and Butch Marshall are two of the best people ever to walk the earth. Thank you for being part of our family.

Lisa Anderson introduced us to each other and has been a great friend to the two of us ever since. Thank you so much, Lisa. We both owe you a debt we can never repay.

•

GREG HERREN WOULD LIKE TO THANK:

Michael Ledet, for opening his home and his wonderful screen porch to me, and thereby making it possible for me to eventually come home much sooner than I could have ever hoped. I love you, Michael.

Timothy J. Lambert and Becky Cochrane progressed through

the aftermath from online friends to real world friends. They, too, opened their home to me and made me feel welcome. And Becky's husband, Tom Wocken, is also worthy of mention—if for nothing else, for getting me a Whataburger when I was too lazy to go get one myself.

Jean Redmann and everyone at the CAN office: Mark Drake, Seema Gai, Darrin Harris, and Tyson Jackson; for giving me a place to go every day and friends to look forward to seeing. Thanks guys, I will always treasure the memory of those first months after we got back—especially the dime martinis at Bacco.

Mark Richards and Johnny Messenger, for making sure I was never lonely after I returned to New Orleans.

My coworkers at the Haworth Press, for their love, support, and concern.

Lee Pryor and Julie Smith, for always being good to me.

Chuck Brooks went from being a nice guy to being a dear friend in those dark months in late 2005. Thanks, Chuck, you have no idea how much it meant to me.

Marika Christian, on whom I can always count no matter what crazy things happen in my life.

•

PAUL J. WILLIS WOULD LIKE TO THANK:

Karissa Kary, for her efficiency and endless energy, and for our trip to Silver Dollar City, where she got me to ride the Powder Keg. You're my best friend and I love you.

Ed Able, for being there through so many difficult situations in my life. Thank you for playing so many roles for me—mentor, friend, and "Dad." The escapes from reality are so needed at times.

Thomas Keith, for calling to check in each week to make me laugh, and for sending me books when I had none. I know you're a friend to count on in any situation.

Joshua Holmes and Marty Hyatt, for their persistence to keep in touch and develop our friendships further. Your thoughtfulness, concern, and creative energy are greatly appreciated.

My friends and coworkers at the Tennessee Williams/New Orleans Literary Festival for making sure that the event would continue amongst the chaos, providing a welcome diversion, a purpose, and an avenue to get back to New Orleans.

introduction

IN THE WEEKS AND MONTHS that followed Hurricane Katrina and its horrible aftermath, those of us who lived there staggered through life like zombies. Many were displaced with no home to come back to—and even now, some are still without homes. When Alyson Books came to us with this project, we were of two minds about it. It was a difficult decision to make; and working on it was enormously difficult. It was hard to read essays about what people had been through, just as it was difficult to read essays about what we were beginning to think was a "lost world."

Yet as we began to assemble the writings collected here, we soon found that the pieces we were getting were as eclectic a mix as the city that we loved and hoped would be back. And doing it from a queer perspective was, we felt, rather important.

New Orleans was a beacon of light in a conservative region for many queers, who fled their birthplaces for her welcoming arms. She was the first Southern city (and one of the first nationwide) to recognize domestic partnerships and to offer partner benefits. Southern Decadence was one of the longest running gay celebrations in the country, and the city always recognized and protected *Southern Decadence* from attacks from fundamentalists. There was never a gay ghetto here; queers were a part of every neighborhood in the city, and rainbow flags proliferated. This is not to say that homophobia didn't exist here; it did, and still does, as it does everywhere in this nation. But at the same time, the city's mentality of *live and let live* prevailed—a system of tolerance that was truly the American ideal.

Within these pages you will find different viewpoints about our fair city, from Pastor Dexter Brecht's brief write-up of the fire at the Upstairs Bar, which triggered the queer rights movement in New Orleans, to J.M. Redmann's harrowing tale of flight and grief, to Greg Herren's interspersing of his blog and diary entries in the fall/winter of 2005 with his own personal history of the city. There are brilliant pieces from respected poets like Martin Pousson, Kay Murphy, and Jewelle Gomez. We've tried to reflect the diverse make-up of the Crescent City with the pieces assembled, and we hope that the differing styles can give those who love our city from afar a better idea of what our city is about—and why it is so important that New Orleans recover from this terrible tragedy.

The unique beauty of New Orleans has inspired artists, musicians, and writers from the earliest days when the French decided to settle in the crook of the river in the early eighteenth century. New Orleans has a heritage of culture that most cities would envy. Making a list of writers who have drawn inspiration from New Orleans would have to include such amazing literary luminaries as William Faulkner, Tennessee Williams, Sherwood Anderson, Ellen Gilchrist, Frances Parkinson Keyes, Shirley Ann Grau, Walker Percy, John Kennedy Toole, Truman Capote, Anne Rice, Stan Rice, Christopher Rice, Patty Friedman, Christine Wiltz, Julie Smith, Tony Dunbar, James Sallis, Poppy Z. Brite, Patricia Brady, Nancy Lemann, Richard Ford, Sheila Bosworth, Jason Berry, Greg Iles, Ace Atkins, Erica Spindler—and that's just scratching the surface.

Make no mistake, New Orleans will recover from the devastation. It will be a long and arduous process, but we have a long tradition here of recovery and survival.

Laissez le bon temps rouler encore!

—GREG HERREN AND PAUL J. WILLIS

a westerner ponders
new orleans

a foreword by patricia nell warren

WHEN I WAS A LITTLE KID in the 1940s, I first met the
city of New Orleans as a powerful and mysterious spirit who had
reached all the way into the Pacific Northwest and touched her
finger into the cemetery in my Montana hometown.

The Hillcrest Cemetery was located in hayfields and rolling
hills west of town, near the county airport. It was "neutral belief
territory"—the result of a recognition by the growing town of Deer
Lodge that things had to get less bigoted on the interment front.
The Catholic Church, whose Jesuit missionaries had occupied
the ground floor in local history, originally had the only cemetery
game in town, but they were sticky about allowing people of other
religions, or no religion at all, to be buried in "their" territory. So
everybody in town took a deep breath, and relocated Catholic
graves out into the ecumenical sweep of agricultural land, where

they now rested cozily among Baptists, Anglicans, Reformed Mormons, Freemasons, Christian Scientists, and atheists.

Two of the oldest graves belonged to nameless early-day settlers from New Orleans. How did local historians know this? Even though Montana is a semi-desert climate and the water table was deep below ground, these were traditional New Orleans burials—the coffins set above ground with a tomb built over them. One was boxed by weathered brick, with mortar crumbling out. The other was a rectangle of native porphyry quarried in the mountains long ago.

When my family visited the cemetery on Memorial Day to decorate our plot, I always felt the pull of those two anonymous burials—the mystery of those forgotten lives. I'd slip away from the opulent Victorian part of the cemetery, where my German immigrant great-grandparents and great-uncle and the rest of their generation slumbered beneath massive granite memorials amid the shade of lush cottonwoods and weeping birches.

Out in the hot sun of that oldest part of the cemetery, I'd stand there pondering those two weathered piles. The area around them was bleak, untended—no nice green lawn or planters full of pansies. But Mother Life had gentled the graves in wild baby's breath just coming into bloom—it had seeded itself from florist bouquets across the way. The seeds had probably walked over here on the shoes of previous curious visitors. The cemetery maintenance man had given up trying to battle the baby's breath—it was now considered an ornament, not a weed.

My newborn writer's imagination tried to grasp the enormous journey those two men had made. They may have been of French descent, maybe even Cajun or Creole, and found their way up the Mississippi to St. Louis, and from there laboriously up the Missouri with a boatload of voyageurs. They came at the end of the fur-trade era, just before the Montana gold rush filled the Rockies with greed, insanity, and violence.

I already had a sense of myself as being "different," and wondered whom they had loved. Were they straight? Did they marry tribal women, as so many pioneers did? Were their wives buried there somewhere too, amid the baby's breath blowing in the wind, under some of the toppling anonymous wooden crosses or eroded stone markers in that same area? Did they maybe love each other? After the beavers vanished, these men might have made a living as free traders, or perhaps joined the small community of mixed-blood stock raisers in the Deer Lodge valley, dealing in Indian-bred horses and the first tricklings of Spanish and American cattle coming up from the emigrant roads.

I was struck by the cultural stubbornness of their graves—planning for a high water table in a country where rainfall averaged only nine inches a year, where drought is frequent and severe.

The deed hinted at New Orleans's hold on her children. No matter where they emigrated, they took something of New Orleans with them. She was an urgent spirit, very passionate and possessive of her progeny—so different from the benign post-Christian traditions that had sent so many European and Eastern immigrants to sleep there, whose burials were all framed in a generic conformist post-Victorian style with brooding stone angels.

When I grew up and left Deer Lodge, New Orleans was one of the many things that stuck to my shoes like some of those tiny baby's breath seeds. She went away with me into my future as a writer.

•

EVERY GREAT CITY HAS HER powerful spirit who guards her walls and tends her public life and her people's destiny. In Athens, she was seen as warlike—Pallas Athena, a battle-maiden armed with shield and spear, driving a chariot and four careening horses. In Rome, she was Juno, stately, motherly, a diva of commerce, her temple guarding the mint where Roman coins were struck. In

London, she was Themis, keeper of the law, riding her river on a great barge. In New York City, she is Liberty poised on her island, balancing a book and torch.

The Spirit of New Orleans might be called a *loa* or a goddess, and given different names, depending on whom you talk to. She is tinged with the color of many peoples, black, brown, and white, who built on that high ground above a swamp, by a great natural port. Her toga may be draped in the same European neoclassic style that inspired many of her older buildings, but it's an African textile. Her necklace is Mardi Gras beads. Her shield luminesces with fish scales. After all, she's a harbor girl.

Today, in these post-Katrina times, she has her work cut out for her.

Whatever her name, she was the American city who sent her children out as carriers of traditions that stuck to their shoes no matter where they went. Early-day black jazz musicians fanned out to Chicago and New York, and took their music with them to create a sound that ultimately defined an entire nation and every skin color in it. New Orleans cuisine went out to the world—all Americans know the taste of gumbo and pralines, and they're learning other dishes too, as Emeril Lagasse celebrates the city's culinary inventiveness on his TV show every day. New Orleans was first to export that decorating trend called "shabby chic," conveying an image of frayed but enduring gentility.

Last but not least, New Orleans writers, whether Tennessee Williams or Anne Rice, Mark Twain or Kalamu ya Salaam, gave a gift to Americans of prose with an urban pungency of narrow old streets where the drains don't work too well, and the gardens are recklessly overgrown. Historically the city has been a refuge for writers, an inspiration for them.

Many of our more straitlaced American citizens sniff at NOLA, at her festering poverty and feisty decadence, at her year-round calendar of pagan festivals, whether it's the saturnalias of Mardi Gras and Southern Decadence, or the spiritual sensations of

Voodoofest, or the Satchmo sounds of Jazz Fest. They brag that they have their roots in a more Puritan and proper and prosperous port somewhere else—in Boston or Philadelphia or Seattle. A few cities can argue that they are the oldest in North America—St. Augustine, Florida, and Santa Fe, New Mexico. The pueblo of Acoma, New Mexico, alleges to be the oldest continuously inhabited site, with people living under its viga beams since 700 A.D. and a guardian goddess with corn silk in her headdress. As someone who is part Native American, I can claim a root or two in Acoma. But New Orleans has a richly layered history that is unique—a mingling of languages and bloods and sexualities and sensibilities, even a commercial transcendence, that places it on the short list of the great ports of the world, the ones that last almost forever. She is a peer of Rome, London, Constantinople, Hong Kong, yet nothing like any of them.

There is a little of New Orleans in everything that's American.

For me, New Orleans is the only city in America where I knew I'd been there already when I finally arrived.

•

IT WAS THE LATE 1990S when I first visited the city. New Orleans Pride had invited me to be its grand marshal. I stayed with a Pride committee member in his Garden District home and got my first whiff of the storm drains in the Quarter, the noise on Bourbon Street, the bustle of the waterfront, the chicory coffee at Café du Monde.

I was not surprised to realize that gay people had gathered in New Orleans from the very beginning. The port had drawn us there in wave after wave, on Spanish galleons and French frigates and American square-riggers and modern-day cruise ships of all nations. We have always been numerous among sailors. We have always swelled the ranks of travelers, of refugees looking for a more liberal land. Often we carried the coats-of-arms of aristocrat clans where we were protected from social censure by family wealth and power. It is no accident that the oldest gay bar in the U.S. is Lafitte's on Bourbon Street. It is no accident that there are gay krewes in Mardi Gras. In a very real way, the deepest roots of gay, lesbian, bisexual, and transgendered life and liberty in the United States must be looked for not in New York or San Francisco, but in N'Awlins.

We were cautiously made welcome in New Orleans, I learned, because we brought jobs and dollars and tourism to a city where these were precious. All the grim anti-gay machinations of the Religious Right, who have such power in the South, have failed (so far) to dislodge us from our longtime niche in N'Awlins. Economics creates its own inarguable measure of tolerance.

After the Pride festival ended, I was taken to restaurants, museums, antique galleries, voodoo shops, and of course the de rigueur visit to the St. Louis number-one "city of the dead." There I paid my respects to Marie Laveau, and walked around for a long time, reading the names on tombs, feeling that feeling of childhood time coming full circle. Lo and behold, on one of the other tombs, I found my family surname. A distant relative of mine rested there, bones crumbling just above that murky water table so close to the surface. My Warren forebears were originally from West Virginia, a genetic blend of English Quaker and Melungeon, but they had scattered through the South and West—this was the first I'd known that they'd wandered clear down to New Orleans.

With time I would return to the city several times for Saints & Sinners, the only literary festival I know where the workshops and panel discussions take place in bars.

Attending Mardi Gras a few years ago, I enjoyed an ineffable trip up the river as part of an RSVP cruise aboard the *ms Zuiderdam*—a chance to approach the city the way the Native American canoes and Civil War privateers had done, and now the oil tankers and container ships anchored in the roads approaching the harbor. It's no surprise that today I remember the river trip more vividly than

Mardi Gras.

The moment came when I told my friends I was thinking of moving to New Orleans someday, to live there for a few years and really get to know the city. I did take note that my New Orleans friends were nervous about the levees. They talked about the "big one" the way people in L.A. talk about the "big one." Only the big one in NOLA was going to be a hurricane.

•

AFTER MOST OF NEW ORLEANS flooded, I anxiously tried to keep in touch with my NOLA friends who were now scattered everywhere from Florida to Chicago, refugees again, but not from hate this time—parked here and there with friends and family across the South and Midwest. The Internet was the easiest way to reach them, and little by little I found them all. Friends who lived in the Quarter managed to learn that their homes had survived more or less unscathed.

In those first days after Katrina, the Religious-Righters announced that they knew for sure, beyond a shadow of a doubt, that God had destroyed New Orleans because the city tolerated gays.

"Then God's aim must be terrible," a friend of mine said dryly. "He destroyed the whole Gulf Coast too, and a lot of non-gay people."

A year later, as I write this, America still faces our government's lack of care for the countless thousands of people whose lives were lost, whose health, homes, and businesses were destroyed by Katrina. The Iraq war shows our disregard for people of other countries, but Katrina puts such a glaring spotlight on our government's apparent inability to meet the urgent human needs of American citizens.

Our government not only forgot about the people and the city of New Orleans—it also shot itself in the foot by forgetting about the Port of New Orleans, fourth busiest in the world and vital to the U.S. economy. After Katrina, the port was dead in the water, cranes toppled, workers vanished. Gary LaGrange, president and CEO of the Port, told *Forbes Magazine*: "Congress has developed a case of amnesia now that the national media has moved out of the city. They have forgotten about New Orleans." Many months later, as I write this, the port is still struggling to get fully operational again.

Great cities pay a big price for living such long lives—they go through cycles—power and glory, then death and destruction and extreme hardship. In the early centuries of this era, ancient Rome was hammered by invasions and almost became a ghost town, its population reduced from millions to perhaps 50,000 people. It was several centuries before Rome slowly began recovering and rebuilding and repopulating itself. In 1666, most of London was destroyed by the Great Fire, as a direct result of government failure to recognize that most of the medieval wooden city was a potential firetrap. It took nearly half a century to rebuild London. These are times that test the spirits of not only the people of the city, but even the City Spirit herself.

The Great Lady of New Orleans surely had tears mingled with rain running down her cheeks as she surveyed the devastation of her city and her people after Katrina. While she can't prevent the downturn cycles from happening, she guards the secret of rebirth and new life.

Today New Orleans's most precious export to the rest of the country will not be music or cuisine. It will be a renewed consciousness of America's urgent responsibilities to its own people. Not since the 1960s have such great numbers of American citizens been marching and demonstrating and protesting about urgent human issues. But today nationwide protest is finally happening everywhere—touched off by the immigrant issues, the Iraq war, the blatant corruption in our public and corporate life, the growing loss of civil liberties, and most of all by our country's seeming abandonment of its historic position as a world leader on human rights. Katrina-related protest expresses an outrage against political apathy and blundering, against the greed of insurance companies and land-grabbing developers, against deliberate attempts to disenfranchise the people of color across the North Gulf.

New Orleans has asked America a fateful question. Her spirit is reaching far, far into the American mind, the way she did across thousands of miles into my home town, and she is touching millions of hearts and minds with a horrendous and heartbreaking question about America's future—not only as a democracy, but as a country where every human life is supposedly respected.

Can America answer that question?

•

WRITERS HOLD A KEY TO that wracking question that New Orleans has become. Words are needed, whether the editorials expressing outrage, or the stories touching millions of hearts.

There is no doubt in my mind that New Orleans will rebuild. Even as the floodwaters were finally receding, people were stating their intention to go home and rebuild. Among them were events producer Paul Willis and author Greg Herren, my friends, who announced that the Saints & Sinners Literary Festival would happen as usual in May 2006. There is no doubt that the port will be repaired—at enormous expense, of course—for the simple reason that the U.S. can't afford to write off a major port.

With government apathy still so glaringly obvious, citizen activism is stepping in. As I write this, 700 college students who had volunteered for debris removal are in St. Bernard Parish as part of a Habitat for Humanity project. TruthOut's Allie Deger, who went with them, said: "When I asked the students why they chose to spend their spring break gutting out houses in Louisiana rather than lying on the beach, they all shared the same lament:

We cannot rely on this government, this administration to provide assistance to its citizens."

Will the *new* New Orleans be the warm humanist multicolored pulsating port city that it always was? Will it be a rebirth of the familiar city that dreamed awake all that jazz and wrought-iron balconies and the Jell-O shot? Will the street musicians and shrimp fishermen come back? Will Mardi Gras really be the same as before? I wonder. The new post-1700 London was not the same city as the old medieval London, but it became equally powerful in a new and unique way.

Will the spirit of New Orleans be driven away, so that those who value money more than human lives can build a cold tight-ass anti-ethnic anti-humanist post-millennial hub for big business?

Whatever the future holds for New Orleans, this anthology is part of that rebuilding. Those of us gay people who live in the city, and those of us who don't but who are the city's spiritual, more distant children, are part of that future, whether the Religious Right likes it or not. Our hopes and dreams get quietly tracked everywhere, like baby's breath seeds on people's shoes. We pop up everywhere, in the damnedest places. We're impossible to eradicate, impossible to resist. Like New Orleans, we are an irresistible, indestructible part of America.

There are new stories that only we can tell, and new ways of telling old stories that only we would know how to find.

desire

FOR THE STREETCAR*

jewelle gomez

Today I saw Desire
darkly painted steel, hard bells
wheels and unseen motivation.

Here, in the morning traffic
she is thick with patches and paint
antique convenience keeping to the track
lumbering alongside palm trees
not the Mississippi

*SAN FRANCISCO HAS RENEWED STREETCARS FROM AROUND THE WORLD
ON THE FAMED MARKET STREET LINE TRAVERSING THE CITY.

Little hints at her bewitching scents
lost in the change of locale,
night's restless forces still
a mist on her skin or
the heat-driven engine that
is her name.

Speeding past are
cars full of assumptions
careless, surface motion
not sensing the dervish of want
in their midst.

This time I will be refuge,
a stranger keeping the promise,
kindness remembered,
touching my hand to the flame.
Not drawing back.

freedom's just another word for nothing left to lose

TENNESSEE WILLIAMS'S BAPTISM OF FIRE IN NEW ORLEANS

dr. kenneth holditch

SEVERAL SIGNIFICANT WORDS RECUR IN all of Tennessee Williams's remarks concerning his life in New Orleans: He often termed the city "one of the last frontiers of Bohemia," in which he felt at home because he considered himself a Bohemian. Perhaps the most significant word that he uses often is *freedom*, as when he asserts that it was in New Orleans that he first found a freedom he had always needed, "and the shock of it against the Puritanism of my nature gave me the material about which I continued to write." The freedom that he encountered in the Vieux Carré in the late 1930s took several forms, ranging from such a simple manifestation as a change in his style of clothing to a complete revamping of his attitude toward sexuality in general and his own sexuality in particular. By his own admission, he arrived in the city dressed in a coat and tie, attire to befit the grandson of an Episcopal minister, and when he left, he was wearing open-toed sandals and a Hawaiian shirt, a change that reflected what had occurred in his attitude toward life in general. He was liberated from the constraints of his troubled family life: the tumultuous marriage of his parents, the disdain his father directed toward him, and the rapidly deteriorating mental balance of his sister Rose. The freedom to which he referred was all-encompassing, involving the physical, mental, and emotional elements of his life and work. His background in Mississippi as the son of a prudish mother and grandson of an Episcopal minister, in whose rectory he had spent his early years, produced a proper young gentleman, at least on the surface, however much passion might boil beneath. The New Orleans freedom also involved a release of those passions, and he very soon adapted to that lifestyle and embraced it as his own. The quotation from Hart Crane's "The Broken Tower" used as the epigraph for *A Streetcar Named Desire* reflects the mental, emotional state of Tom at that time:

> And so it was I entered the broken world
> To trace the visionary company of love, its voice
> An instant in the wind (I know not whither hurled)
> But not for long to hold each desperate choice.

The release of his pent-up sexuality in an area where the gay life was, if not condoned, at least not generally condemned, contributed much to the flowering of his career.

I do not mean to suggest that the conversion of Williams's character occurred suddenly, within the few months he was in the city in 1938 and 1939, but rather evolved, albeit rapidly, over a period of five or six years, during which he left and returned to

New Orleans several times. At the end of that time, the young, proper poet Thomas Lanier Williams had become Tennessee Williams, and even the adoption of that *nom de plume* reflected the loosening of the ties that held him to his Protestant upbringing. The freedom that he encountered was not just the well-publicized and often exaggerated sexual license ascribed particularly to the French Quarter but a way of looking at all aspects of the human state that reflected a *laissez-faire* approach to life, to some degree a result of the Latin and Caribbean component of the city's history and population. There is an old saying in the city: "People in New Orleans don't care what you do, but they want to know about it."

A happy concurrence of events brought Thomas Lanier Williams to New Orleans in December 1938. If he had not hated St. Louis enough to flee, or if he had acquired a WPA job in Chicago before turning his eyes South, the playwright destined to produce some of the greatest American dramas might never have developed— and *A Streetcar Named Desire* might never have existed. The first visit awakened the impressionable young writer's mind and spirit to the unique nature of the most European of American cities. He professed in later years to have been astounded by what he saw in the old French Quarter, where the Bohemian enclave established among writers and artists in the 1920s had melded with the easygoing, laid-back attitude and lifestyle of the mostly French, Spanish, and black population to produce one of America's most interesting cities. Writers Sherwood Anderson, William Faulkner, Carl Sandburg, and Oliver LaFarge, among others, had resided for varying periods of time in the Vieux Carré, the old town in what Anderson called "America's most civilized city." Anderson insisted that what distinguished New Orleans from other American cities was the fact that imagination was given precedence over facts. For the Ohio novelist, always in full flight from the midwestern values of his childhood, the word "civilized" surely covered not only the power of imagination, but also the individual's freedom to pursue the pleasure of the flesh, from food and liquor to sexuality in its variety of manifestations. And it freed the author to write about subjects that would have been verboten in other parts of the country in a non-judgmental way that was something new in American fiction.

By 1938, most of the famous authors had moved on and the Quarter was no longer the hotbed of creativity it had once been, but artists and writers still lived in the area, where rent was cheap, food was delicious, and the easygoing Latin attitude provided them an atmosphere in which to flourish. Tennessee's comment about the encounter between freedom and Puritanism that the city afforded him reflects much the same attitude as that of Anderson, Faulkner, and their contemporaries. On January 1, 1939, he settled into the first of several rented rooms he would occupy in the region, this one at 722 Toulouse Street, which would four decades later become the setting of *Vieux Carré*, a memory play about his early days in the Crescent City. In 1946, Tennessee moved with his companion Pancho Rodriguez into the third-floor apartment of a building on St. Peter Street, and it proved to be his favorite dwelling in the Quarter. In his study was a skylight, under which he could sit at a refectory table and work on *Summer and Smoke* and a play to which he had given various titles, including *Blanche's Chair in the Moon* and *The Poker Night*. From that apartment, he could hear the streetcar named Desire, which ran through the Quarter on Royal Street, two doors from his building, and then back Downtown along Bourbon. Six blocks away, the Cemeteries streetcar lumbered along from the river to graveyards a couple of miles away. As a result of this happy accident, he renamed the play *A Streetcar Named Desire*.

As usual, whatever he was working on, he wrote as if driven, from early morning till afternoon, when, "spent with the rigors of creation," he would go to a favorite Quarter haunt—Victor's Bar and Restaurant, Galatoire's, or Antoine's—for drinks and lunch. Then he would walk to the New Orleans Athletic Club for a swim, after which he would wander, sometimes sitting with friends in Jackson Square, observing the life there. Many places he saw became symbols in his play: the French Market, in those days an open market where farmers from outlying regions sold their produce and stalls in which the freshest shrimp, fish, crawfish, and crabs, all of which the dramatist loved, were for sale; Saint Louis Cathedral, whose bells would become a major image in the play; and of course the ubiquitous, noisy streetcars rumbling through the narrow streets of the old city. How could a poet not be inspired by such a locale?

And the inhabitants of the Vieux Carré! At home was the volatile Pancho—he once cut up all of Tennessee's clothes in a temper tantrum—and in the streets Bohemians and outcasts, who were, he always felt, his own clan. In later years, he would tell his friend, journalist Don Lee Keith, that seeing Ruthie the Duck Girl, one of many local characters, had reminded him that "in New York, eccentrics, authentic ones, are ignored. In Los Angeles, they're arrested. Only in New Orleans are they permitted to develop their eccentricities into art." One can still imagine Blanche DuBois lost in that world, a stark contrast to that in which she had lived. One night, years later when Tennessee was walking toward his house at 1014 Dumaine Street with Don Lee Keith, they observed a spot in which a tourist had been robbed and killed. Keith remembered that "Williams thrust his hands deep into his blazer's pockets, stiffened his elbows, and took a half dozen or so unsteady steps before delivering the pronouncement, 'Well, I'd still rather be killed in New Orleans for money than in Los Angeles for thrills.'"

Vieux Carré is the play in which Williams traces the impact of the freedom afforded by the city of New Orleans to the young, basically innocent, aspiring playwright. The setting is a seedy rooming house on Toulouse Street, much as it was, he informs us in the stage directions, when he lived there in 1938 and 1939. The *dramatis personae* represents a cross section of the French Quarter residents at the time, the end of the Depression, for the most part, down-and-out victims of a social system that has consigned them to a low station with no opportunity for advancement. The central figure, the consciousness through which the events of the drama are conveyed to the audience, is a young writer, "myself those many years ago," Mrs. Hortense Wire is the cantankerous landlady; and there is a struggling and desperate artist, Rossignol (Nightingale), who insists that he is part of an old Louisiana family. There are two elderly ladies, Miss Carrie and Mary Maude, faded gentry, so impoverished that they eat out of garbage cans, a fact they would never admit; despite the fact that they are, the writer says, "dying of malnutrition," they are at work on a Creole cookbook. And there is Jane Sparks, a failed fashion designer from New York, who is dying of some undisclosed disease, and Tye McCool, her lover, a young stud from Mississippi, who works as a bouncer at a Bourbon Street strip joint. On the ground floor is the apartment and photography studio of T. Hamilton Biggs, a society photographer, who also makes for himself "art pictures" of "young drifters" in the Quarter. Then there is Nursie, the black servant who does most of the work in the rooming house and takes care of Mrs. Wire, whose grasp of reality is tenuous at best. Nursie is perhaps the most clear-sighted and realistic of all the inhabitants of the crumbling old townhouse, as demonstrated in the scene in which she talks to Jane, who is so moved by the plight of Miss Carrie and Mary Maude that she plans to buy them "a sack of groceries at Solari's" but fears that such an act may injure their pride. Nursie replies, "Offend 'em, did you say? Honey, they gone as far past pride as they gone past mistaking a buzzard for a bluebird."

The overtly dramatized loss of innocence and concomitant gaining of freedom comes in the seduction of the young writer by Nightingale, who enters his narrow room one night. He observes that the writer's face "is still youthful as your vulnerable nature" and pronounces him "a victim of conventional teaching, which you'd better forget." After the writer confesses to Nightingale that he has recently lost his virginity to a paratrooper, the painter performs a sexual act on the supine writer, urging him to "lie back and imagine the paratrooper." Following the two sexual initiations, the writer imagines the apparition of his grandmother, recently deceased, who appears in the alcove opening off his room: "And as I drifted toward sleep, I wondered if she'd witnessed the encounter between the painter and me and what her attitude was toward such perversions? Of longing?" It seems to him that the spirit of his grandmother is lifting one hand as if in "forgiveness? . . . through understanding?" and he is at peace. Thus the writer has been freed of the Puritan society's strictures against such sexual acts and of the necessity to please the family member he loves the most. The episode with the paratrooper, by the way, comes directly from Tennessee's own experience, at least as he recounts it, and the advances of Nightingale may be autobiographical or perhaps rather a dramatic device to enhance his drama.

Observing and listening to Jane and Tye, the writer is introduced to a sphere of intense, consuming sexuality that he had never known existed. Tye's remark to Jane—"you got a lot to learn about life in the Quarter"—is a succinct statement of the theme of *Vieux Carré*. Even Tye, to all appearances a corrupt and corrupting influence, exhibits to Jane "faintly innocent—boy's eyes."

After a short period of time, Mrs. Wire observes the alteration in the young writer: "You've changed since you've been in this house. You know that?" The writer agrees and acknowledges that he has "some troublesome little scruples" in his makeup that present problems in his "negotiated—truce with—life." What he has learned in New Orleans, he adds, is that everything has its price: "For everything that you purchase in this marketplace you pay out of *here!*" and he indicates his heart. One night Mrs. Wire pours boiling water through a hole in the kitchen floor to break up a party in the photographer's studio, and they all end up in night court. The writer is called to testify. When asked if the landlady had committed an act of "malicious mischief," he evades the question by saying that he thinks it "very unlikely a lady would do such a thing." After Mrs. Wire is fined fifty dollars, she confronts the writer with having betrayed her, then offers him a drink. She speaks of the ghosts of people who have lived in her house and of the oppressive loneliness which she must endure: "I heard some doctor say on the radio that people die of loneliness, specially at my age. They do. Die of it, it kills 'em." The slightly intoxicated young writer, having pondered the people he has met in the house and the events he has witnessed and the words of Mrs. Wire, concludes, "God, but I was ignorant when I came here! This place has been a—I ought to pay you—tuition." This scene brings to an end the first half of the play, and already the protagonist has acknowledged that he has been educated by living in the decaying old townhouse among the outcasts of society.

Part Two of the play essentially dramatizes what it is the writer has learned and is in the process of learning from his sojourn in the Vieux Carré. It begins with the writer's composing a passage that, although he rejects it as mere "exposition," sums up the nature of his education: "Instinct, it must have been directed me here, to the Vieux Carré of New Orleans, down country as a—river flows, no plan. I couldn't have consciously, deliberately, selected a better place then here to discover—to encounter—my true nature." Mrs. Wire, who views the Vieux Carré as "the new Babylon destroyed by evil in Scriptures," despite her cantankerous nature and deliberate acts of cruelty, feels maternal toward her young tenant and endeavors to direct the course of his life, presumably unaware of his sexual orientation, but he rejects her control, saying that he did not "escape from one mother to look for another." (Ironically, in a later scene, when tourists on a garden tour come into the patio attached to the house, one of them calls the other "Edwina," which was the name of Tennessee's mother.)

The young writer learns something from each of the inhabitants of 722 Toulouse Street. Nightingale instructs him in how to get free medical treatment by seeing a doctor, then refusing to acknowledge the bill when it arrives, and presumably he does just that, since he has cataract surgery even though he is living on nickels and dimes he makes in tips as a waiter in Mrs. Wire's restaurant. His sexual education continues when he tells Mrs. Wire that he hears Jane "crying" in her alcove and the landlady replies, "That woman's moaning in there don't mean she's in pain," to which he replies, "I never heard sounds like that." Later, listening to Jane and Tye's lovemaking, even as he writes about it, he comes to realize that "writers are shameless spies." As he prepares tentatively to leave the rooming house and the French Quarter, he is instructed by Sky, the clarinet player with whom he will head west, on the life of a vagabond. Sky tells him that they will siphon gas from other cars to power his and that "we'd have to exercise our wits. And our personal charms." Sky, by the way, is based on Jim Parrott, a friend Tennessee first met in 1939 in New Orleans, and the two of them did indeed travel to California and remained friends for the rest of the playwright's life.

The range of the writer's education, the degree to which he has achieved freedom from the constraints of his youthful life, is indicated in a scene between him and the painter. Nightingale, in his tubercular and emotional agony, wonders why God, who has "moral obligations," is allowing him to suffer, and the writer, who by this point has moved outside the parameters of his religious upbringing and added a certain cynicism to his view of life, replies, "I think that morals are a human invention that he ignores as successfully as we do." The young Tom Williams must have come to believe in those early Quarter days, as does the writer in the play, that "there's nothing either good or bad but thinking makes it so," or, as Hanna Jelkes expresses it in *Night of the Iguana*, "Nothing human disgusts me unless it's unkind, violent." In Nightingale's view, the writer's education at the hands of the Quarter has made him "rock-hard as the world." To which the writer, who recognizes in his nature two inherent elements at war with each other, "the storm of my father's blood" and his grandmother's "tenderness," replies, "I had to survive in the world," indicating the microcosmic nature of the Vieux Carré in the lives of the drama's characters.

Finally, *Vieux Carré* clearly demonstrates that the French Quarter has provided not only inspiration and material for the young dramatist, but it trained him, if we accept the evidence of *Vieux Carré*, to be the great creator that he became. The protagonist, late in the play, sings:

> Makes no difference how things break,
> I'll still get by somehow
> I'm not sorry, cause it makes no difference now.

Determined, as the lyrics indicate, to proceed with his life no matter what must be changed, broken, what compromises he must make between his dreams and ideals on the one hand and harsh reality on the other, he abandons 722 Toulouse, proclaiming, "I've grown into a man, about to take his first step out of this waiting station into the world." As he departs, Mrs. Wire cautions, "Now watch out, boy. Be careful of the future. It's a long ways for the young. Some makes it and others git lost," and he replies, "I know." He stands by the door, "frightened of it" because "to open it is a desperate undertaking. . . !" and the man who then steps through that door into the streets of the future is radically different from the innocent who first entered it.

Vieux Carré—a much better and more significant play than most critics have realized—dramatizes effectively not only the impact of the city on young Tom Williams but also many of his feelings about his "spiritual home," as he often referred to New Orleans. He once called it "that gregarious city," an acknowledgment of the friendly camaraderie among residents and outsiders, particularly in the French Quarter, but he was well aware of the negative aspects of what Jane calls "this corrupt city." Much as he might embrace its lifestyle, he always reserved to himself a certain disdain for the licentious nature of life in the Quarter. Early on, his mother has been troubled by the fact that he was being exposed in New Orleans to low-life elements, to those who existed outside the boundaries of what she considered polite society, and finally Tennessee himself to some degree moved toward her attitude, speaking in 1978 of the unfortunate decline of morality as exhibited along Bourbon Street. Yet he could speak of it lovingly in such a remark as, "I've never known anybody who lived in or even visited the Quarter who wasn't slightly intoxicated—without booze." Through all the years of his association with New Orleans, 1938 to 1983, the city remained for Tennessee a mecca, a place where he could allow his spirit, wounded by the barbs of New York film critics, to heal; where he could rest and draw his breath; where he could replenish his creative energy. It might not be a kind city to Blanche DuBois, but for her creator, it was ideal.

As to what Tennessee might think of New Orleans post-Katrina, could he view it—as perhaps, who knows, he may be doing somewhere from the pantheon in the great beyond—he would certainly not align himself with the evangelists and politicos who carelessly dismiss the man-made catastrophe with the assertion that it emanates from God's wrath toward a "new Babylon." Tennessee did not condemn human beings for the sins of the flesh, to which all are heir, but rather for their sins against one another, their "deliberate cruelty," which, as Blanche DuBois observes, having herself been guilty of it, is the one unpardonable sin.

Ah, yes, thank God Tom Williams came to the French Quarter in 1938, for there he was transformed into that miracle we call Tennessee Williams, and he became the spokesman for his generation, especially for those, who, like him, were outcasts from "polite society," the "fugitive kind," as he labeled them.

He was our Virgil, our Dante, our Shakespeare. The rest is theater and literary history.

cocksucker suit

poppy z. brite

[T]he thing I love about New Orleans is that it tends to be deserted, and there you may find peace. It is in the quietude, the deserted streets, the green and eccentric palms. Shortly after five o'clock the business district is deserted, and you won't find a person on the streets, except for one fellow in a seersucker suit. He will be walking slowly down Gravier Street, smoking a cigar. Tending his own garden. —Nancy Lemann, *The Ritz of the Bayou*

ROUND ABOUT LAST MAY, I started wanting a gentleman's suit. I'd never owned one before, and at first I thought I wanted a big-shouldered superfly suit in green or maybe dark purple, like the hip-hop stars and NBA players wear. All this changed the day I went to lunch at Mandina's, the crusty, classic Creole restaurant on Canal Street in Mid-City. I don't remember what I ate—probably soft-shell crabs amandine—or what I drank—probably Wild

Turkey—but I'll never forget the fat man in blue seersucker who bellied up to the long bar, or his friend who came in, clapped him on the shoulder, and said, "Hey, Frank! I see you're wearing your COCKSUCKER SUIT!"

From then on, no other kind of suit would do for me. It had to be a cocksucker suit, and it had to be from Perlis, the iconic Uptown clothing store.

One of the strangest evenings of my life had taken place at Perlis that January. New Orleans sports broadcasting legend Buddy Diliberto, who taught me more about my home city than anyone aside from John Kennedy Toole, had just died. Caught in a tizzy of grief and nostalgia, we were on our way out the door to his visitation when my friend Doug Brinkley called and said, "Hunter's about to go buy a seersucker suit at Perlis, and he wants to meet you."

I was never sure how these two things were connected, but I'd been reading Hunter S. Thompson since I was fourteen, and though my obligatory days of trying to imitate his inimitable style had long since passed, he remained a major influence on my work and general outlook. Doug, his biographer, had been promising to introduce us for years, and I really wanted to go. Still, I was on my way to a wake. . . . "Could we have dinner later in the week?" I said.

I don't remember how Doug replied, only that something in his tone made me suspect if I didn't meet Hunter that night, I might never meet him. So we went tear-assing up to Perlis on Magazine Street, dressed inappropriately in the Saints gear we'd put on for the wake (and would wear to it, after this). Perlis was closed, but Doug had apparently secured Hunter a private fitting. And there he was, a tall old Kentucky-faced man in smoky glasses and loud pants, looking like nobody else in the entire world. Of course he had an entourage: his extremely beautiful young wife Anita, Doug, and another young man who seemed to be designated solely to hold his glass of bourbon. I'd no idea if he knew who I was, exactly, but he hugged me, kept asking my advice on which seersucker suit to buy (in the end he got both), and kissed my hand when I told him I'd take him somewhere good to eat while he was in town. It never happened, and a few months later, depressed and in constant physical pain, he shot himself dead.

There was that memory, and there was the part of my personality that had become a hidebound old Uptown doyen, worshipping Rex, chowing down at Commander's Palace and Clancy's, muttering dire imprecations against the newfound trendiness of the Lower Ninth Ward. I don't like to indulge that part of my personality too much, but I figured I could buy him a suit. Maybe even a couple of ties. And I knew he'd want to shop at Perlis.

The plainest truth I can state, though, is that right around my thirty-eighth birthday I became almost unbearably tired of doing female drag. I'd done it most of my life with varying degrees of comfort, mostly because I thought I looked "better" that way. I was no longer so convinced of that, and anyway I'd lost most of my interest in "looking good" if I had to be deeply uncomfortable in order to do so. I had dresses I liked—the flamingo print, the vintage swing dress, the '70s knit halter top—but more and more often I found myself wearing plain black cotton trousers and a Hawaiian or oxford shirt. I spent most of my time looking like a parrothead or an off-duty waiter. If I was going to dress decently without dressing like a girl, I needed to get myself some more dignified gentleman's clothes.

They didn't know quite what to make of me when I went in for my fitting at Perlis. At first they could not be dissuaded from the idea that I needed the suit for some sort of restaurant job (I've since noticed that Café Adelaide does, in fact, dress its servers in seersucker, though not full suits of it). When they realized I just wanted it for myself, they fluttered around in dismay—"It's not possible! It won't look right!" I'm pretty sure they were looking for a polite way to say my ass was too big to wear men's pants, but I tried on the smallest off-the-rack size and demonstrated that this was not so. I finally convinced them to sell me a $200 suit by telling them that when my husband saw how good it looked, he'd want to get one too. For whatever reason, "husband" seemed to be the magic word; I guess it was acceptable to sell a suit to a cross-dresser as long as it wasn't an actual *pervert* (though if the man who actually rang up my purchase was heterosexual, I am Shaquille O'Neal). I did not mention phantom penii, gay men in female bodies, or nonoperative transsexualism. A week later, when the necessary alterations had been done, I was the proud owner of a Perlis seersucker suit . . . and the Uptown-street-tiles tie, too.

•

From my journal, May 19, 2005:

The cocksucker has landed! I went to pick it up shortly after 1:00 P.M. today. The tight-assed gentlemen of last week had been replaced by an older lady who loved the whole deal: "What a wonderful idea, hon! I might have to get me one of those!"

I had to take Chris to work before I could come home and try it on, which is probably just as well: This is going to take some experimenting and getting used to. I felt funny when I first put everything on. I'm not used to buttoning up collars or tucking my shirts in, but more than that, though I've certainly worn men's clothing before, I've never actually gone whole hog on the cross-dressing thing. I stood in front of the mirror wondering if I looked ridiculous. Probably I do, and will, at least to some people, but this is something I want deeply and that means a lot to me personally; although it's fashion, it's not entirely (perhaps not even primarily) about how I look. The suit, however, is beautiful. . . . I've never worn a tie before and haven't yet got the hang of tying one, but with the help of my printed-out eHow directions, I'm figuring it out. I have amassed a variety of beautiful button-down shirts (mostly from the Salvation Army, I'm afraid) and tried all of them on with the suit. I'm embarrassed to say that, thus far, I like it best tieless, with a blue Hawaiian shirt that has bomber planes and bikini girls printed on it. You can't entirely take the parrothead slob out of the man, I guess.

•

I DEBUTED THE COCKSUCKER SUIT at Commander's Palace and made Chris take lots of pictures of me standing against the interestingly textured cemetery wall across the street afterward. My favorite of its public appearances thus far, though, came a few weeks later when I went to meet a friend for lunch in the Quarter. He was (and is) a distinguished gentleman of literary bent, and when he opened his front door, I saw that he was wearing . . . *a seersucker suit*. We matched!

We went to lunch at Antoine's and had Sazeracs (him) and Old-Fashioneds (me) and soufflé potatoes and oysters and brandy, and he proceeded to drink me under the table, and when I staggered out to put more money in the meter, a family of tourists gazed at me with big, wonder-filled eyes. I couldn't figure out what they were looking at until I remembered I was wearing the suit *and* the Uptown-street-tiles tie. I had one of those moments, simultaneously irritating and gratifying, where you realize you've just given the *turistas* a taste of precisely what they expect from New Orleans, maybe without even knowing they expect it—in my case, an obviously cross-dressing person, obviously tipsy at 2:30 in the afternoon, tottering out of Antoine's with bourbon on my breath.

Unfortunately, the 2005 hurricane season trumped the end of seersucker season. The cocksucker suit survived, though, and hangs in the closet of my currently uninhabitable home, needing only a good dry-cleaning before I bring it back out this May. Some of my discomfort with female drag has receded—I've had bigger issues to deal with this year than my lifelong gender dysphoria—but I still look forward to putting it back on. No matter what changes are wrought upon New Orleans, it helps to know that as long as the city remains even vaguely habitable, I will be able to walk into a cool, high-ceilinged restaurant any time between May and September and see a man in a cocksucker suit. Possibly I'll even be looking in the bar-back mirror.

greyhound boy, 1976

martin hyatt

ONE DAY, WHEN I AM thirty or maybe thirty-five, it will happen. I will feel the need to tell the story and the story will have to start somewhere.

New Orleans is that somewhere.

I am five or six or something like that, and I can't remember what day of the week it is, or what month it is, but it is kind of cold. And it is the first time in my life when I feel like running away.

Being that I am five or six, it must be 1975 or 1976. And my immediate family is like this: a mother, a father, a sister, a brother, me. And of course, being that it is the mid-seventies, we are all riding in a blue station wagon. And being that we are poor, it is sort of falling apart. There is always the fear that the car will overheat again, that the muffler will fall off. Something like that always happens. Going from Covington to New Orleans, a 50-mile drive, is risky in a car like this.

My father is driving; my mother is holding my baby brother,

James, in the passenger's seat. I am in the backseat wondering how deep the waters of Lake Pontchartrain are. I have never been much of a swimmer; I am more of a drowner. It's as wintry as it gets down here, and the heater works, but not too well, and my brother is throwing some sort of a fit. After several weeks at Children's Hospital, they still can't seem to find out what's wrong with James. My father tends to believe that he's fine, that there's nothing wrong with him. But I see that look in my mother's eyes every time my brother cries, like it's a cry that a good mother like her is supposed to understand, but she cannot. My father is staring straight ahead as we cross the long bridge into the city. He doesn't say much to my mother these days. I can see her reading his mind sometimes. She kind of has to do everything.

My mother turns away from James for a moment and points out the buildings on the horizon. "That's New Orleans, kids," she says. "That over there is New Orleans." Then she looks out at the water. I wonder if she thinks of drowning too.

I can see the buildings in the distance. From where we are, they look gray, like they are not really there. Like they can just disappear. Years later, my best friend Michael and I will be teenagers and we will drive across this same bridge with other boys, drinking beer, searching for ourselves amongst men deep in the heart of the city. We will make our ways from our run-down houses and trailer parks and become the most glamorous boys dancing on the tables of the bars of the French Quarter. We will feel rich. We will be royal. We will become faggots in the city that will let us dance even after dawn. New Orleans will become ours. It will be beautiful. It will feel a lot like love.

But today, I'm still a kid and we are heading into the city because my father, Martin, same name as me, has to go to the V.A. hospital. It's not clear what's wrong with him either, if anything. But like all of his brothers and sisters, my dad has something wrong with him that can't be determined. It'll be something that requires all kinds of tests and medical visits, but it will end up being something seriously unserious.

My father is too old to be my father. He's at least fifty-two and he is way too old to be the father of a three-, a six-, and a nine-year-old. My half-sister, Sheila, is already in her twenties. There is something about my dad that is barely there. It's like he died after one of his other marriages, after his first wife or second wife walked out on him. And now he's a shadow of what a father should be. When I see my mother touch him, it's as though her hand goes right through him. My father is behind the wheel, but this station wagon is driving itself. Maybe we will all drown.

There is a brief moment when James stops crying, when the song on the radio is one that I like so much it makes me move around in my seat until I find just the right position to listen to it. "Some people wanna fill the world with silly love songs. . . ." I know that at church they told us that the Beatles said they were more popular than Jesus and listening to them is a sin, but I think that maybe Wings is okay. Besides, I like the song so much, even the possibility of burning in hell will probably not stop me from listening to it.

The city is visible now. We never really do anything exciting once we get to the city. It's the ride that is the excitement, the pleasure. This sort of trip lets me pretend that I am really going somewhere, like we are going to someplace more than a hospital. But I know that's all it'll be. And we'll top it all off with dinner at Burger King, so I can get one of those paper crowns that I can never put together just right.

Every time we go into the city, every time from my window, I see the world of New Orleans. And I long to reach through the glass and lay down on the streets and let the trumpets from the musicians on the street corners put me into a sleep where I will dream in peace. From that moment, from the backseat of a station wagon, the streets of New Orleans become my home.

Even when James isn't crying, there is tension in the air, knowing that at some point he will start up again. Sometimes I feel that if

I could hold the baby, maybe I could talk to him, figure out what the doctors cannot. Or maybe they could just do it all over again, restart the process and have a James that's like other babies. The fewer words there are between my parents, the more the silence becomes a roar. I sometimes think that I'm the only one who can hear the roaring sound of them saying nothing.

We are traveling through a maze of traffic-filled streets and ramps and overpasses. I want to be having a good time. I want it to be an adventure. My parents aren't like most of the ones in my neighborhood who smoke pot or drink or leave their kids alone or let them starve. My parents are always with us. But they are never with each other. They are in the same places, but never together even when they are together.

My sister, Lisa, across from me in the backseat, is reading a *Little House on the Prairie* book. It's one that my mom just finished reading. They read a lot, my mom and my sister. And my sister is bossy about everything, and I make fun of her. She's pretty and she knows she's pretty. In a few years, people will start to tell her she looks like Brooke Shields, and later Valerie Bertinelli. And it will be true. Lisa's still mad at me for tearing the arms off her life-size doll she got for Christmas. I don't know why I did it. I found it under her bed, was just playing around with it, not seeing it as a doll at all, but just a piece of plastic. I didn't want to tear it apart. I wanted to see how it was put together. I do this with my own things too. My trucks, my pinball machine. I take them apart, tear them apart, thinking that I'll understand how they work better if I see what's inside. But I can never put them together the same way.

Once we reach the hospital, there is the expected fuss between my parents about which street to park on. And fifteen minutes later we are piling out of the car to escort my father to the doctor. My father seems tough and healthy for a ghost. I thought doctors were for the sick.

Instead of Burger King, we go to the hospital cafeteria. Nothing probably tastes good here, but it all looks like it tastes good. Even the green Jell-O is attractive. So many choices. Maybe that's why I decide to have nothing. I've learned to like the way it feels to say, "I'm not hungry," even when I am. I like the way it gets my parents worked up. I like the way the world seems to stop when I say I don't want anything to eat.

My dad is having some sort of test done, and my mom and Lisa and my never-content brother eat while I venture just far enough away so that I won't get in too much trouble. Just far enough for my mother to say, "Don't go any farther."

I stand by one of the windows of the hospital and even at this age, I know that when you are on a high floor, it is possible to jump. I don't really want to, but I like knowing that I could if I wanted to. The world below is quiet. Nothing moving. Then I see a line of people walk from a building down below to one of several buses. "Where are those people going?" I ask my mother.

"That's the bus station, honey. I don't know where they're going."

"Away," I say to myself.

The people are all dressed differently. Some look like they are going to fancy parties and others look like they just got out of bed. They are black and white, some look happy and some look like they would have jumped from one of the windows up above if given a chance.

"Son, get over here. You have to eat something."

I ignore her. The bus with the long, skinny dog on the side is going to pull away, taking all those people someplace they've never been. I wonder how old you have to be before you can leave on a bus with a dog on the side of it.

There is a black man by the bus station with a trumpet. He smiles in a way that I wish my father would. People getting off buses, getting on buses, are creating changing small crowds and listening to him. I want to go down there. If I could jump without hurting myself, I would.

And I would join the crowd, except I wouldn't leave the

musician standing on the corner alone. I would stay out there, maybe forever. I would live with him. I would fall asleep on the pavement to the sound of his trumpet.

I can tell that the music makes him sleep like me. I see that look in his eyes when he looks at the buses like he can't decide whether to get on one or not. He really knows how to dream. He doesn't know who I am, but he is my friend.

I want to go down there. Next time we come to New Orleans, I'll have to plan ahead and pack a bag. I'll come and live with my new friend.

"Son," my mother pleads. "Come eat."

I'll have to wait until next time. I go over and to please my mom, I finish off a hamburger. Lisa's reading her book again. James starts to cry. My mother looks exhausted, tired in a way that no person should ever have to be.

In the car, on the ride home, I know I am in the wrong vehicle. I feel like a hitchhiker picked up by this family from the Northshore. This is my family, but I am supposed to be living with those strangers, those musicians. I will eat music for dinner.

Yet, I am here in the station wagon. I'm disappointed and angry, and if I knew how to swim, I would get out of this car and swim miles across the lake back to the city.

I am sad now, but from my window, I see a bus. It is passing us like it's going somewhere other than the Northshore. I don't understand why anyone would want to leave New Orleans to go to places like Covington. Then I realize that a bus just like this one probably moves just as smoothly from Covington to New Orleans. As soon as I get home, I will pack my belongings, and I will walk to the bus station and get on one of those buses.

I will leave my family behind, but I will not be afraid. I will find friends like me: dreamers, lovers, artists. I know from an early age that my home still waits for me somewhere else. Somewhere just beyond the horizon. New Orleans.

café reflections out of the blue

karissa kary

IN A POST-KATRINA NEWS REPORT about New Orleans, I heard: "The rest of the city is in ruins, but the Quarter pristine."

No one who ever set foot inside the Quarter before, during, *or* after the storm, would describe it as pristine. The twisted street signs, broken glass, worn-down buildings, streets littered with garbage and donkey manure from carriages carrying well-dressed and well-fed tourists—all a matter of form. And of course there is the unforgettable bouquet of vomit that drifts off of Bourbon Street on particularly hot days. Charming, perfect, unique, quirky—yes. Pristine—never, from any account I have seen.

The Quarter suffered no flooding but there are physical reminders everywhere. It doesn't take long to become acclimated to them. Here, there is no water line, though there are the people, and the people wear their water lines everywhere they go. Even now, seven months after Katrina in this "pristine" Quarter, limbs still hang low and broken, and blue roofs dot the horizon. On most days I do my best not to notice the irregularities. Not out of ignorance or to turn a blind eye but out of a need for normalcy on some level.

•

I NOTICE THAT THERE ARE fewer people than normal at the café as I sit down and open the paper to a special section inserted inside. The headline reads "Out with the blue and in with the new. Everything you always wanted to know about replacing your roof." I flip through the section and realize I already know more about roofs than I ever thought I would. My own roof suffered minimal damage. Three different times roofers have come to my home and fixed the damage and yet I still set up pots around my house when it rains to catch the water that drips from the ceiling.

The newspaper has been left in a pile with others in front of me. A bearded man with glasses sits nearby while I flip through. He answers his cell phone and at some point in his conversation I hear: "The new roof is going on next week; the electrician left yesterday." I stop reading the comics and find the roofing section immediately. I put it on his arm and he stops talking to see what I want. I say, "Here, it's all about roofing." He reads the headline, thanks me and then tells his cell phone friend his good-luck find. A young man sitting across from us interjects that his uncle is a roofer and currently overloaded with business that he can't finish because he is working on his own family's home. I nod sympathetically.

I start to go back to *Doonesbury*, and am interrupted by the young woman at the next table who has perked up from her textbook to somewhat timidly say, "New roof? What was it you said?" I peel through the pile of papers in front of me and find another roofing insert to hand her. "Yes, that's what I need for sure.

Halfway through." I nod and say, "Good luck." A very pregnant woman walks directly in front of me and hovers there as she shuffles through the remaining paper stack to very deliberately find another roofing section. She succeeds, sweetly nods at what has become the roofing convention seating area of the café and waddles off to read. I look around before I pick up the rest of the paper and note that beside me there are seven people seated in this portion of the café and I now know the status of four of their roofs.

The next headline tells me that in Gulf Coast hurricane destruction, "Louisiana damage tops the list," and leads into an article about recovery which reads, "The garbage is to go on a new schedule to enhance efficiency after complaints throughout the city that garbage had been left to rot on curbs for weeks." Fewer than eighty days of pre-hurricane season hopefulness remain and in that time twenty-three mayoral candidates will have their say in what will be rebuilt. I put down the newspaper and look out the window. A man walks by wearing a shirt that reads, "For Lent, I have given up hope." I wonder if his home still has a roof, and how long his garbage has been on his curb.

As I walk out of the café I laugh at myself as I notice the loose shingles on the café roof. I read a large sign on the building: "Delivering you the genuine LA taste experience. Welcome Home." Indeed. I'm glad to be back.

storyville

melinda shelton

USING A DRUNK'S GPS, THE bum in wrinkled khakis, his blackened cuffs dragging through Bourbon Street soup, zeroed in on his target. His laceless Adidas looked like bloodstained casualties from a Jimmy Connors/John McEnroe rumble in Flushing Meadows. "Pabst Blue Ribbon Is Always Pure" stretched to the tearing point on a T-shirt that didn't begin to cover his bloated, hairy beer belly.

Just as Sister Agnes taught us in eighth grade, I crossed the street to avoid Trouble with a capital T. What the nun didn't teach us before a class trip to Sin City is what to do when Trouble followed us to the other side.

Thirty yards and closing. Twenty. Ten. I cut back across the street, pleased with my last-second tactic. With nary a misstep off the sidewalk and over the gutter, PBR Man deftly maneuvered in front of me. He was a thirsty pro, bent on getting his next frothy fix, and I was his Sugar Mama.

A sweaty hand smacked against my forehead, snapping my head backward. The surprise move stopped me in my tracks. My Girl Scout bravado withered. Mama always said I was courting Trouble by moving to New Orleans, and sure enough, here he was in Technicolor and stinking to high heaven.

"My GAWD, Mel! Your weirdo beacon's going off again, girlfriend. COVER IT UP!!!"

His palm still covering my forehead, Lucas grinned and took a long drag off the straw protruding from his 32-ounce attitude-adjusting daiquiri. There's nothing quite like a drop-dead-gorgeous gay man playing hooky in the French Quarter on a weekday afternoon. With his boss. "Girrrrrlllllll, he's got the eye for you!" Lucas growled and emitted a low wolf whistle. So macho, that man.

Undeterred by this amateur street theater, PBR Man stopped a foot short of my nose. Lucas stiffened, although it wasn't Tea Dance Sunday. It looked like I would have to rise to the occasion and save our tushes.

I dug into a pocket in my classic Gap jeans and dragged out a fistful of quarters, dimes, and nickels. Street people are as much a part of our city's landscape as tarot card readers, drunken tourists, and drag queens. So, I always carry loose change to fill my Random Acts of Kindness quota.

I dropped the coins into the grimy hand floating dangerously close to the ta-tas Lucas gleefully pointed out to total strangers—usually women—when he was tipsy. He giggled and winked. Jesus H. Christ.

Mind like a cash register, PBR Man rang up the change. He handed back a couple of coins. Nickels. "Too much trouble." I apologized and offered up two more quarters. As a bonus, I threw in a couple of Marlboro Lights and my Bic lighter. Cha-CHING!

Trouble crossed the street, his GPS guiding him to the nearest tavern, which in the Quarter doesn't take long. Lucas grabbed my arm and we dashed for safety at Good Friends. A couple of Cosmos later, our street encounter forgotten, Lucas transformed himself into Samantha and entertained me with his true-life-embellished adventures of Sex in the Crescent City.

New Orleans is the mother lode, a genuine storyville unlike any other in the world. Live here, and you are required to create and collect stories, real and imaginary. Need proof? The PBR Man story is true, Lucas is real, and despite a storm that left thousands in limbo, somewhere, someone is having sex in our city.

•

FOR MANY OF US, NEW Orleans provides anonymity when we need it, or serves as an outlet for raucous, raunchy behavior at Mardi Gras and Southern Decadence. Here, we are a community of educators, doctors, writers, cops, lawyers, artists, soldiers, business owners, parents, and lovers. We are also activists who demanded seats and sat at political tables we once were only allowed to serve.

It has taken us decades, too often at great cost, to arrive where we are today. Police raids and newspaper stories of arrests for lewd behavior, or some other trumped-up, demoralizing charge, cost people their livelihoods and their lives. Ask Charlene Schneider, the legendary owner of Charlene's on Elysian Fields, what public outing did to her career. Or Ellen DeGeneres, who cut her comic teeth on Gay Pride audiences in Washington Square. Call forth the spirits of those murdered in the streets and in their homes, or in a burning bar, and ask them about the ultimate price they paid so those of us who followed can work and live and love in New Orleans. And remember the too-many felled by AIDS, a deadly virus heralded by hatemongers as God's vengeance against homosexuals.

Some of us were lucky enough to be born and raised in New Orleans. But many of us came because we were lured by Fate, a temptress far too beguiling to ignore, or we wanted to be part of the rich lesbian, gay, transgender, and bisexual history that is undeniably New Orleans.

One of us answered a classified ad.

•

FAUBOURG MARIGNY: OCTOBER 26, 1998.

This couldn't be it. I must have the wrong address. Omygod, let it be the wrong address. I circled the block again: Burgundy to Frenchmen to Rampart, past Charlene's, to Elysian Fields, to Burgundy.

The landscape hadn't changed in the three minutes since I'd last seen it.

What the hell had I done? Left a cushy, nice-paying P.R. job in Washington, D.C., that's what I'd done. Plenty of benefits, sixth-floor view of the Silver Spring Metro stop. A bar in the basement. Everything a middle-aged gal could want.

An ad in the Sunday *Times-Picayune* classifieds section kick-started this whole story: "EDITOR needed for an established New Orleans newspaper." I called, dazzled the boys with my lengthy resumé and newspaper-writing awards, and was offered the job at half the pay I was making.

Just like that, I became editor of *Impact*, a mostly biweekly lesbian and gay newspaper I had never laid eyes on. I lied in the interview and said I was quite familiar with the paper, a regular reader, as a matter of fact. Turns out, I confused it with *Ambush Magazine*, which is a different story for another time. All I knew was the job was my ticket to New Orleans.

"YOU'RE GOING TO DO WHAT?!!! Are you CRAZY?!!! A"—gasp, sputter—"GAY newspaper?!!! You'll ruin your career!!! No other real paper in the nation will take you back!!! People will think you're gay!!! What about teaching? You'll never be able to teach again!!!"

Her voice dropped, pleading over the telephone: "Please tell me you're kidding." I regretted checking into a smoke-free hotel room in Princeton, New Jersey, where I was on a P.R. junket for my D.C. employer. Already in the doghouse, I fired up an illegal Marlboro Light and watched the smoke permeate virgin ceiling tiles. Nope, I wasn't kidding, I said. I was coming home. It was a leap of faith.

The discussion was not unlike one we'd had several years earlier when I suffered wanderlust, and in a matter of five weeks left Baton Rouge and took a job in D.C. With a suitcase, two boxes of essentials, and no place to live, I flew out of Louis Armstrong in a driving rainstorm on Fat Tuesday. I swore I'd never come back. Obviously, that's not how the story ended.

So here I was back in New Orleans on a beautiful fall day, sitting gape-mouthed in front of a shotgun double with peeling gray paint, an arm's length away from what appeared to be a flophouse at best, more likely a crack den. A pair of athletic shoes, laces knotted, dangled from the power lines at the corner. I'd read enough big city murder mystery novels to know the shoes meant a murderous gang had the corner covered.

My leap of faith felt more like a dive into an abyss.

I knocked on the screen door. There was scraping on the other side. Muffled voices. Locks disengaged and the door opened. "New editor's here, y'all. Come see!" Great. I was a sideshow freak.

Introductions were made: Kyle the former owner who sold *Impact* to a gay newspaper chain; Lucas the designer; Chris the office manager; Tommy the ad salesman and singer in the gay men's chorus. All boys. I dropped the "Dip me in honey and throw me to the lesbians" lapel pin into my briefcase.

It was Lucas who made a lasting first impression with his jet-black hair, milk chocolate eyes, and gorgeous smile. "Hey, there!! I'm Lucas. What's your sign? Oh, Virgo, that's GREAT! I'm a Taurus and we get along great with Virgos! It's Melinda? Anybody ever call you Mel? Mel it is! We're gonna work great together, Mel!"

First and last time I ever wanted to be male. What a hunk. It was the beginning of a beautiful friendship.

So began my life in New Orleans as editor of an LGBT newspaper. We changed the name to *Impact News* to speed the transition from borderline bar rag to a newspaper that would appeal to the entire community, gay and straight. We painted the building a cheerful yellow to contrast nicely with the crack house next door, and expanded into the other side of the double. Determined, we snapped the death-grip bar owners and ill-tempered competitors had over gay publications, took the paper weekly, and broke into mainstream advertising and distribution. *Impact News* became the award-winning LGBT newspaper New Orleans deserved.

•

"HELLO, HELLO, HELLO! ANYBODY HOME? Ah, yes, Ms. Editor! I'm Roberts Batson—some people call me Bob—and I write the gay history column for the paper AND I conduct gay heritage tours in the French Quarter. At your service, ma'am."

Roberts Batson entered my life carrying a go-cup and tugging on the leash of a large dog named L'Enfant.

"I'm here to take you on a tour of the bars that distribute our fair newspaper. There are some ugly people out there who think this new WOMAN LESBIAN editor has two heads! Yes, indeed, this is true! You need to, shall we say, charm the pants off those who only WISH they had two heads! I'll be back in two hours and we'll be off!"

I had no clue how many bars there were in the Quarter, Marigny, and Bywater. As we entered an establishment, Roberts whispered: "Brief stop, no drinks," or, "Major players, schmooze, have a cocktail." Six hours and far too many cocktails later, even *I* thought I had two heads.

Roberts's energy and passion for his vocation—writing about the city's rich LGBT heritage and conducting his acclaimed "Gay

Heritage Tour" in the French Quarter—continues. Roberts, who refuses to call himself an historian, *is* an historian, a devoted collector and preservationist of our stories past and present. For decades, he has lived and breathed our heritage, marched in the streets, worked in politics, and taken tourists on his compelling tour. Most recently, he returned to the stage with a brilliant one-man show: *Amazing Place, This New Orleans*.

It is Roberts who is amazing. Without people like Roberts, our community would have remained underground, chased there by hate-filled homophobes who have never given up the pursuit.

There are so many other remarkable people who made *Impact* the important community voice it was, beginning with Roy Letson, who started the paper in 1977. According to Roberts, the early editors were Roy, Gary Martin, and Jon Newlin. Charlene Schneider, who opened her bar as a refuge and community meeting place, also contributed to the newspaper. Roy sold *Impact* to Kyle Scafide in 1992, and Jon remained editor for several years.

Roberts began writing his "Claiming Our Past" column in 1994, which is when he also launched his tour. Roberts says he recommended to Jon that Marilyn McConnell join the staff to write about and for the lesbian community. For the twentieth anniversary of the newspaper in 1997, Roberts wrote a year-by-year retrospective, including profiles of twenty-one LGBT community leaders. Another longtime writer was Ed Real, who left the paper in 1999.

During my three-year tenure as editor, I worked with phenomenal women and men who, like Roberts, became my family. These people, and the entire community I came to respect and value, fueled my desire to work, live, and love in New Orleans:

Lucas Mire, my cohort, talented designer, and certified celebrity hound. Margaret "DJ Mags" Coble, our music writer, Dyke March promoter, and my next-door neighbor. Marilyn McConnell, whose "Lesbian Voices" column was the lifeblood for the lesbian community. Woe to anyone who denigrates women in Marilyn's presence. Greg Herren, our fitness and health guru, whose fitness column provided a workout for every position. What I still cannot understand is how he looks so damned good with a cocktail and cigarette in his hand. Ron Williams, our brilliant artist and dear friend. We were crushed when Ron moved to Santa Fe in search of a less hostile climate and more spiritual energy center. Death came too soon to this very special man. Mike Theis, who proved an Uptown guy could sell ads for a gay newspaper and still find a date. Dale Boggs, our office manager who made Martha Stewart look like a pansy. And Robby Picou, a salesman who took Lucas's place as the man in my life. As men so often do, they left: Lucas for Atlanta and Robby for San Francisco.

I cannot forget the many restaurant critics, who literally did work for food, and community-minded souls who reviewed books and films and freelanced for very little pay, if any. And there was Ray-the-delivery-guy, who made sure *Impact* and *Eclipse* were delivered each week. He is another fine man who left us far too soon.

Then there were the men of *Eclipse*, a slick, sexy publication that satiated every gay man's prurient side. With bylines like "Rod Steel," the guys wrote about everything from leather to gay porn to drag queen advice for the lovelorn to clever coverage of the raucous New Orleans nightlife. Phil, Phil, Phil, how I miss your racy repartee!

There are countless others who invested in *Impact News* and *Eclipse*, including Cleo Pelleteri, our landlady and proprietor of the Claiborne Mansion. When I arrived without a place to live, Cleo generously opened her home to me. She is a very special woman, indeed.

The end of *Impact News* came when its misguided owners in D.C. and Atlanta insisted on merging us with their Atlanta paper. I and my staff argued how New Orleans is a completely different city, and how the paper had survived for almost twenty-five years. We asked them to meet with community representatives and advertisers and listen to their ideas. Our pleas fell on deaf ears. As we fearfully predicted, the paper sputtered and folded. It was a sad—and completely unnecessary—loss for our community.

•

ASK ANYONE WHO LIVES IN New Orleans. There's something in the water, some mutated organism that embeds in whatever lobe controls our ability to think and to speak, and we become bards who wax poetic with our tales of the city, some true, some mythical, some both.

Storytelling is part of our community. Not lying, mind you, but the art of relaying a story based on fact, perhaps on rumor, with a sobering moral or a side-splitting punch line. There is reverence when a story commands such, or drama queen theatrics replete with colorful language and exaggerated mannerisms. Liars, and there are many, stew from the sidelines where they plot a way to slither back into grace—or into someone's bed.

My love affair with this wonderful and deeply wounded city continues. New Orleans beckoned to me when I was a child, entertained and educated me as a college student, and welcomed me as a newspaper reporter and editor mesmerized by its people, traditions, and its inexplicable and miraculous ability to survive adversity.

I fell in love on my first visit to the city in the summer of 1967. To my parents and brothers, it was just a vacation, hardly a life-changing journey. However, I was enchanted the moment I planted my eleven-year-old butt on a Rampart Street stoop. The sights, sounds, and people in this magical city so far from Shreveport beckoned to me. When I told my mother that I'd live in New Orleans someday, she smiled and nodded. She, too, believed.

Little did I know that sultry summer, some thirty years later I would call New Orleans home. I fell in love with Shawn, who has jet-black hair, milk chocolate eyes, and a gorgeous smile. In May

2004, Shawn and I bought a bungalow in Mid-City, where I finally had a stoop to call my own.

Our lesbian, gay, transgender, and bisexual history in New Orleans is a story in progress. Self-appointed, godless homophobes like "the Reverend" Grant Storms and his soulless lemmings have failed to stamp "The End" to our saga. Likewise, a storm named Katrina may have scattered many of us to the winds, some never to return, but most of us will follow our storyline back to this city that embraces us.

On August 29, 2005, broken levees shattered lives and thrust our beloved city and people into chaos. We grieve for the lives lost and for friends and family who are struggling to return. Shawn and I and thousands of other nomads from our precious community will live elsewhere until the government rights a terrible wrong, and we can rebuild our lives.

Inevitably, when once again New Orleans calls, we will answer and come home. Unwritten and unspoken stories are waiting.

living in desire:
a new orleans memory

for Greg Herren, B.D.L., and J.P.

victoria a. brownworth

DESIRE IS A PLACE IN New Orleans, a shadow neighborhood. Desire is also nights in New Orleans, endless nights of endless seeking. Desire is a metaphor for the city.

Having been raised by a pair of liars in a family of liars, it was inevitable that I would find my way, early on, to the city of liars, the city where truth is as mutable and permeable as the levees: New Orleans.

In a city of liars I could be a different person every day if I wanted to be—and in New Orleans that is what I most often wanted: to be someone else. And so I was. In the city of liars anonymity reigned. In New Orleans no one knew me; I was invisible and amorphous and I could find myself, literally, and lose myself, just as literally. Persona is like a Mardi Gras mask in New Orleans; unmask yourself and reveal the new mask beneath. Lose the old you, don the new you, never reveal the real you. For New Orleans is also a city of mist and ghosts and the two often meld together in the long, fog-shrouded nights and one can so easily disappear into that swirl of oblivion.

•

MOST PEOPLE THINK OF NEW Orleans as a playground, and it is. But New Orleans is also a chameleon town, home to those little lizards who live everywhere and change their skins to match their surroundings. New Orleans is all things to all people. The city of reinvention. The city that time forgot. The city where the good times are always rolling. The most magical city in America. The longest love affair of my life. The city that wove its way into the fabric of my life and heart and became the site of all my wildest dreaming. How I lived in New Orleans, what I learned in New Orleans, changed everything about me, forever.

New Orleans is, quite literally, in my blood, its genetic tracery transmitted from the mosquitoes big as dragonflies that bit and sickened me night after night like small vampires determined to hold claim to me for their city, always.

When I lived there, New Orleans was a place of infinite mystery. Business went on there, yes, but it was mere background to everything else, way down in the CBD, the Central Business District, away from the heart of the city, the place where desire reigned.

New Orleans was all about the mystery—a place of magic and voodoo, of cruel danger and intense poverty, of immense beauty and palpable fear. I arrived there perilously young, semi-innocent and acutely gullible. I was ripe for the taking and taken I was.

There were places I was too naive to know I should not go, a young white girl from the North with an abiding urge to create change and do good, a young white girl who had a hidden and inchoate lust for danger underpinning that other desire to help, mend, and fix. Those desires would clash, day to day, night by night and what got forged was me: reinvented. Changed, as Yeats wrote, "utterly."

New Orleans had that terrible, relentless beauty, the kind Somerset Maugham describes in *Of Human Bondage*, the kind that lures you, that comes unbidden and will not let go, the sort of beauty that can literally take your breath away, make your heart stop.

New Orleans had that effect on me: I would be walking up Prytania on my way to the movie theater, the repertory cinema where I went several days a week, and it was spring—spring comes early there where it is never truly winter—and I would stop still, poised, enveloped, almost as if I were *listening* for it, for that scent of the sweet olive trees already in full bloom. The sweet olive trees with their spindly arms and tiny clusters of creamy blossoms that permeate my senses to this day.

In the North it was still dead winter, but the North was gone for me by then. I was a newly southern girl, with an Alabama accent and a southern sway to my hips and a slower, liquid manner and I would stop in the middle of the street and the sweet olive trees would cascade over me, envelop me in their scent, and I would be embraced by that infernal headiness—stopped still, my breath gone, no heartbeat, my eyes glazed: Just me and that scent, that indescribable, palpable, uncapturable scent, and I would sometimes have to literally cry out from the painful pleasure of the sensation, cry out my love, my excitement, the piercing physicality of it.

For I was by then in deepest thrall. Ready to be held forever in the embrace of all the mesmerizing, ragged, sensual beauty of the place. Its thickness and wetness, fogs so dense that when you looked up at 4:00 A.M. on your way home from the bar where you worked and a man was suddenly there, an apparition from the shroud the night had become, you weren't initially scared, because perhaps he wasn't even real. There were so many ghosts in New Orleans.

But the men who crawled out of the swampy New Orleans nights were always real, and the dangers they held in their loose killer's bodies—the guns, the knives, the just plain fists—were always destined to do you damage. It was part of the payment for being there, for being allowed to languish in the damp embrace of the Crescent City. If the good times were to roll over you, if you were to have your way with New Orleans, then sooner or later one or another of her pimps would come for you and you'd have to pay up.

Yet even bloodied, you'd come back for more. Because that is the nature of obsession and there is no other place in America that can breed obsession the way New Orleans can. It isn't just what it can give you—anonymity, a home in the shadows where you cannot be found by whatever it is you came to escape because it is, above all, a place to which people come to escape—it is also what it demands that you give back. Because in New Orleans, the *gris-gris* must be reciprocal. In New Orleans the voodoo comes in waves and it takes you with it, whether you think you want to go or not. New Orleans is a Faustian town. The dues will be paid. Someone will come knocking—if not for your heart, or your literal soul, then surely for the money you earned that night or the one good thing you own or—something. Because in a city of liars there are inevitably thieves. And in a city of liars and thieves, no matter how in love you are, you simply can't be safe.

•

THERE WERE THOSE WHO SAID just that in the harrowing, heartbreaking days after Katrina hit like nothing had ever hit America in our lifetimes: It was time for the dues to be paid on a city that had laughed its unholy laugh in the face of what everywhere else in the country held dear. It was punishment for all the many sins committed in the arms of the good-time girl of the Gulf. It was God's way of saying how wrong it had all been: Flood the town with water, wash away the sin and decay and guilt and badness and somehow get the place clean enough to start over.

No one who loved New Orleans believed this. Because who but God could have created such perfection, such barely tolerable beauty and enticement? And after all, there they were: The gorgeous spires of Saint Louis Cathedral remained untouched, unrocked, unmoved by Katrina. Somehow that edifice to God that had stood through wars had also stood through the worst hurricane in our lifetime and that meant that God was there, in New Orleans. God had not punished New Orleans. But New Orleans was punished, nevertheless. New Orleans was going down for the third time. New Orleans was on life-support.

What does one do when one's lover has been hurt so terribly? What does one do when there are no bandages, no triage to fix the gaping wound left by so much damage?

One goes to memory, one thinks back on what was and prays that it can be again. Because in memory there is reclamation, in memory there is hope, in memory we can be back in New Orleans the way it was, New Orleans before the last storm hit.

The last storm because there were ALWAYS storms. Storms were to New Orleans like jazz and beignets. Storms punctuated the raucous nights and arrived along with the carillon of the cathedral in the French Quarter every afternoon between 3:00 and 4:00, whether you had an umbrella or not. We knew about storms in New Orleans. We just didn't know there could be a Katrina.

I moved to New Orleans in 1978 never having been there and knowing no one. It was November and I was a fresh-out-of-college girl who had been across country but had never been further south of the Mason-Dixon than Washington, D.C. All I knew of southern heat was Augusts in Philadelphia and the low buzzing of tiny insects and the inertia caused by a thin veil of muggy humidity that slid over the city in late June and evaporated just past Labor Day. I didn't know the South—not even its heat. All I knew about the South was from parents who had been civil rights workers and their black friends who had come North with harrowing tales of lives lived under the harsh rule of racism in Alabama, Mississippi, and Louisiana. The Deep South, the dangerous South, the South to which I had been sent by the domestic Peace Corps (VISTA) to make things—which were still, post–Civil Rights Act, very bad—better.

When I left Philadelphia on that November day it was just below freezing. I arrived in New Orleans with nothing but my Northern woolen winter clothing, a symbol of my naiveté; it was 85 degrees and steamy outside the Kenner airport. I had twelve dollars in my pocket and didn't know that all the payphones took nickels instead of dimes because the South was, in so many ways, in a time warp.

It was the time warp that had drawn me there, a budding journalist and full-fledged activist with several years of urban domestic Peace Corps service behind me in literacy programs and prisons up North. Now I would be a full-time activist for justice, which would start in Desire and Treme, black neighborhoods of whitewashed wooden shotgun houses, rampant illiteracy, and lots and lots of simmering rage.

Poverty and crime are deceptive in the South and most deceptive in New Orleans. Hidden, like the little chameleons that you don't see until they flit across your hand or face and an involuntary shriek escapes you. I knew urban decay in the North: I knew what it looked like, I knew what it smelled like. The streets would begin to decline and then there would be the bombed-out buildings and the vacant lots, the uncollected trash and the graffiti-covered walls. There would be occasional gunfire and the sidewalks would have a patina of broken glass. The confluence of poverty and crime were unmistakable up North—you could literally see it coming.

It was different in the South. Everything had the hazy, gauzy, scrim-shot beauty of a Walker Evans photograph. The edges were blurred and the beauty rose like the heat, from the ground up. I was ill prepared for the malevolence of that beauty and I was pulled into its snare as easily as an insect into a Venus flytrap.

•

IN THE DAYS AND WEEKS after Katrina struck, obliterating the New Orleans I knew, much was said about the poverty and the crime and the blackness of the city as if they were all of a piece and somehow all new, all fresh, all something previously undiscovered.

When I came to New Orleans, one of two thought-we-were-savvy white girls, both of us VISTAs, working for an all-black community project in the all-black neighborhood of Treme, the poverty in New Orleans was crushing. The racism was palpable despite the fact that New Orleans had, even then, a black Mayor, Dutch Morial, a man of Creole descent whose skin was nearly as white as my own, but who was despised by white New Orleanians as fiercely as any "nigra" would be and distrusted by fellow blacks as being in the white man's pocket. Crime in the city was insurgent, the police force the most corrupt in the nation. The standard joke was that it took the police so long to arrive at the scene of a crime because they had to change clothes—from perpetrator to police officer.

New Orleans was beautiful then, as now, even post-Katrina, but it suffered from the same problems: the legacy of slavery and Jim Crow laws, institutionalized racism, epidemic illiteracy and poverty. All of it washed over the city much as Katrina had, seeping into the interstices of the Ninth Ward and the working class neighborhoods like the Irish Channel District where I lived, infecting them all with the spores of anger, resentment and a strange, malodorous inertia that inevitably bred crime and punishment in equal measure.

New Orleans was a *fleur du mal*—a dangerous beauty that lashed out at those who loved her most, a corrupt city whose corruption was so inextricable from every aspect of daily life that it had become as accepted as the storms and the jazz. New Orleans was the most frustrating city in America: incalculably perfect, incalculably damaged.

•

THERE WAS NO STREETCAR NAMED Desire when I lived in New Orleans, nor was there one on my many trips back. Desire was still the seedy neighborhood depicted in Tennessee Williams's play, only now it was poor black instead of poor white. Desire was still code for all that was wrong with the city, code for the contradiction: How could *Desire* be so terrible, so poverty-stricken, so close to ugliness in the midst of such nonstop beauty? How could Desire be bad?

Desire was a metaphor for New Orleans.

Desire went underwater in Katrina.

Desire is no more, a ghost town in the city of ghosts.

Nor is there a Treme. All the little dirty white and pale blue boxy rectangular houses where I used to work, where the little lizards flew out of the drawers and cabinets when you opened them and the black women would howl with laughter when I shrieked every time—all of that is gone now. Obliterated by the full force of the wall of water as it broke through the levees where I used to sit and drink long-neck beers from the Jax brewery nearby, sometimes alone, sometimes with someone I'd just met, because in New Orleans there were always strangers and you were always reinventing yourself with one or another of them.

•

EVERYONE KNOWS WHAT IT IS to be in love, but almost no one can explain it in a way that is neither tedious nor treacly. Suffice it to say I fell hard and fast for New Orleans and like any other victim of a one-sided love affair with a ruffian, I stayed in love no matter how she beat me up, no matter how she failed to change regardless of the endless promises. I left her because I couldn't work with her: The time I lived in New Orleans was febrile and exciting and fraught with danger. By day I worked to effect change in a place that wanted neither change nor knew how to envision it. By night I worked in various bars, as bartender, cocktail waitress, and stripper. I knew every shadow of New Orleans, every bit of the sleazy underbelly that shifted only to reveal more sleazy underbelly. New Orleans was bad to the bone and that was its greatest flaw and its most alluring and enduring charm.

•

IT'S DIFFICULT TO EXPLAIN THE lure of a place like New Orleans for a big city girl who was a born writer. New Orleans has "material" written all over it. There are other cities like that: Los Angeles, Chicago, New York, Miami. Hard, gritty places with little smatterings of elegance here and there. But New Orleans had something none of them possessed: There isn't a square inch of New Orleans that isn't knock-your-socks-off beautiful. From Uptown to the Garden District, from the Vieux Carré— French Quarter—to Desire, it's all one lush stretch of palpable loveliness, a green and fertile delta darling suffused with the scent of camellias and japonica and bougainvillea—enough to make you swoon. There's a foreignness, a strangeness, an implacability to New Orleans that recaptured my heart every day and wooed me into trouble every night. New Orleans is like a big casino; once you start to play the games that await you there, you are lucky to come out alive and you cannot wait to go back.

I left New Orleans to restart the life that stopped when I moved there and I left New Orleans because if I had stayed I would have died; New Orleans was too dangerous a territory for me, too filled with all the allure that a city of liars and thieves begets. My literary

heroine, Lillian Hellman, had had the truth wrung out her there—
only lies were left; another heroine, Lillian Smith, slowly stopped
writing at all, too drunk with the place. And I, I was intoxicated
to the point of poisoning, addicted like a junkie who doesn't care
that all the veins are collapsed and the next shot might be the
hot one. I'm still that full of New Orleans, despite the years that
have passed since the city was my official address. As I said, New
Orleans is in my blood, part of my formal genetics, now. I don't
have to live there to be there.

•

IF YOU'VE NEVER BEEN IN love with a place, you might not
understand, might not get what it is to wake up every morning
besotted by the street where you live, no matter how poverty-
stricken, no matter how crime-ridden. I was homeless for a time
in New Orleans and *still* I was in love. It was just that powerful.

The first place I lived was a tiny house off Magazine below the
Garden District in the Irish Channel. Up the street, on Felicity, was
one of the spots where Louis Malle filmed *Pretty Baby*, the place
where the photographer lived. It was enshrouded, like everything
else untended in the town, by banana trees and ferns. Too tropically
green to be real. An urban jungle from which one imagined long
black panther cats and small spider monkeys might emerge at any
point. One would see a flash of color and think it was a macau or a
parrot, but it was only ever some flaming blossom.

New Orleans is incomparably lush.

I lived in the Irish Channel and I worked in Treme, Desire, and St.
Bernard Parish. None of those places is there now. They've all been
decimated by Katrina and it is hard to imagine they will be rebuilt
because they were the poorest parts of the town and considered by
most to be the darkest and baddest parts of the town, the places
people who lived behind the iron grillwork in the Garden District
or high above the French Quarter wished would simply disappear.

Now those places are flattened and wrecked as if papier-mâché and matchstick houses had stood there. Those places never held any less of my heart than the others. Those were, after all—those places below Rampart Street, below Storyville, below the cemeteries where the dead were always ready to float off in any hurricane or tropical storm and become another phalanx of ghosts in the city's nights—those places were the places that first drew me to the city. Because if New Orleans hadn't been the poor, devastated, crime-ridden, illiteracy-plagued place it was in 1978 (and still was when Katrina slammed it flat), I would never have been sent there.

And had I never gone there, I would never have known, truly, what it is to love with every fiber of one's being. I would never have known as simply and declaratively as I know now that flaws ultimately don't matter to a lover who is utterly taken, swept away. But most terrible of all, I wouldn't have known the beauty that was New Orleans, because it will never, truly, be the same again.

•

SOME PLACES DEMAND SINFULNESS OF their inhabitants. Las Vegas is like that. So is Los Angeles. New York can be, so can San Francisco. New Orleans is a place where people come specifically to be bad, to escape their own inherent goodness—for a day, a weekend, a lifetime. People come to New Orleans to get blind drunk in the French Quarter, to be wooed by the best music in the world, to eat the fattest, most delectable Gulf shrimp, to slurp down oysters and to find someone, anyone, with whom to have the kind of sex only fantasy and pornography promise.

Those who sought answers in biblical admonishment for what Katrina did to New Orleans laid righteous claim to that sinfulness. But in sinfulness, sometimes, lies the purest of joy. And most of the people who come to New Orleans searching for a place to reinvent themselves if only for a night or a dirty weekend are desperately seeking a respite of bliss in the long, slow drudgery of their daily lives.

New Orleans might appear to be the nation's whore, but New Orleans is the most constant of lovers: She will give you everything you want and fulfill every desire you ever thought you had. And then you, like I and so many others, will be in her thrall forever.

•

WHEN THE DISCUSSION OF WHAT to do about rebuilding New Orleans arises, I am never sure of what to say, because there is really only one thing to say: *Put it back the way it was.* When people talk about "better" and "stronger, " "less crime" and "stricter laws" what they seem to be saying is that New Orleans was broken before Katrina hit and now that she's so shattered, it's best to sweep up the mess and start fresh and new instead of trying to piece the broken bits together.

I can't agree with that. Since before the Louisiana Purchase, New Orleans was a corrupt and dangerous town, a town in which crime flourished because of poverty, because of transience, because the rules—what rules there were—followed the Napoleonic Code and were simply different there. But many towns are different from the white-picket-fence heartland image we like to pretend is America and we don't wipe them off the map or allow them to be made extinct. If a huge wall of water hit Detroit tomorrow—one of the ugliest and most crime-ridden cities in America—or The Big One finally rocked Los Angeles, a truly corrupt and soulless town—would we leave these places and the people who live there and leave them to die and just move elsewhere?

History matters, even in such an ahistorical nation as ours. Imbedded in the water-logged shotguns and littered over the flattened landscape of the Ninth Ward and so many other neighborhoods where I used to spend my days in New Orleans is history. Not just my history and this or that person's history, but the history of what made this the most magical, most foreign and most complex city in America.

That cannot be allowed to be obliterated. It's too rich, too immeasurably important to be shrugged away like just so many bad memories.

•

I HAVE BAD MEMORIES OF New Orleans. No one lives anywhere without accruing some bad memories; no place is perfect. But there's balance when a place has your heart as New Orleans had mine and so the good memories always win, always displace the bad.

I have written often of my first Christmas in New Orleans because it was, like Dylan Thomas's *A Child's Christmas in Wales* or Truman Capote's *A Christmas Memory*, an epiphany: It was one of the poorest Christmases of my mostly poor life, yet it was, indisputably, the best.

That Christmas was when I discovered I was deeply, irrevocably in love. I shared a small house in the Irish Channel with two other VISTA friends, B, an attorney from Shreveport already balding, with an inexplicable love of opera and an inability to sing even a single note on key; and J, a woman from Illinois who loved to bake bread and who worked as an organizer in the same office I did in Treme. We were all the same age, all perky idealists with a keenly arrogant sense of our own ability to change the world. It was like a college dorm at the school of hard knocks where we were each matriculating in social activism.

That December we would each come home from our jobs, virtually penniless as those jobs demanded we be, for joining the Peace Corps means taking a vow of poverty: You must live at the poverty level of wherever it is you are stationed. You must live *like* the people for whom you work. So we were all poor. I had gone through my twelve dollars far too quickly and was utterly broke.

So there we were, in the bleak dark of early winter, and I would make us a dinner from whatever we had in the kitchen. B would put Handel's *Messiah* on the little turntable in the dining room. J would get out eggnog and rum and the evening would begin.

For hours we would sit during the weeks leading up to the holiday, every evening that one of us didn't have to work, cutting and pasting construction paper garlands and putting glitter on little Christmas tree cutouts and stringing popcorn and cloves and listening to the *Messiah* with B singing with his heavy Southern drawl and J laughing her rich, heartland laugh.

It was as idyllic as it sounds, the stuff of bad TV movies and worse novels. It was a Norman Rockwell painting and we were each swept up in the mesmerizingly pure joy of it. The season culminated in a standing-room-only, steaming-hot midnight mass at Saint Louis Cathedral. It was my first Christmas away from home, my first Christmas without biting cold or a snowy coverlet outside the church doors. It was the first Christmas devoid of familial obligation and it taught me that alone and family-less I was still okay.

There would be other firsts in that town, some wonderful, like the bawdy grandeur of Mardi Gras, others frightening, like the time I was robbed at gunpoint on the way home from my night job or when I was sexually assaulted by a man lurking outside a lesbian bar on Elysian Fields. But the bad things faded—and there were many—and simply became part of the backdrop of my life.

I was fearless in New Orleans, every day was a new experience, pushing this or that envelope, testing this or that possibility, tiptoeing out on this or that shaky limb. There was nothing I, or one of the various personas I tried on to see how they fit, would not try once in that town, even one evening of Russian roulette with a pair of young Vietnam vets who hadn't lost their lust for killing, guns littering their little house in Bayou St. John.

•

THERE IS A PUBLIC SERVICE announcement for the World Wildlife Fund that notes balefully "extinct means forever."

That is my greatest fear for New Orleans, that the magic I experienced, the breathtaking beauty and subliminal dangers, the ever-present sense that excitement was right around the corner (and it always was), that all those things are on the verge of extinction because there might not be the heart to rebuild what was, because for so many what *was* had a badness to it that they don't want revived.

If you have never been to New Orleans; never spent an evening in the Maple Leaf Uptown listening to ragtime piano as if Scott Joplin had returned from the grave to play it himself; never spent an evening at Tipytina's dancing and listening to Professor Longhair; never eaten biscuits with honey at the Hummingbird as the fat roaches ran across the counter; or watched the chicken frying in a big vat at the Camellia Grill; or had someone whisper to you from a doorway in the French Quarter about voodoo and *gris-gris* and ventured past the cypress shutters into an incense-filled room where a small fat snake slithered around the neck of a veiled Creole woman who wants to take your hand and show you something in the little murky bowl in front of her; then perhaps you don't care if the city is rebuilt as it was, or even rebuilt at all.

If you've never watched the fog rise over Elysian Fields at dawn, or eaten hot beignets dipped in chicory coffee at the Café du Monde, or drunk Pernod with muffaletta sandwiches at the Napoleon House, or heard the mournful bleating of the riverboat foghorns competing with the staccato spurts of saxophone spilling out onto the tiny streets near the Mississippi, then perhaps it is an irrelevance what happens next. If you've never walked through Audubon Park across the street from Tulane (or slept there nights when you had nowhere else to go) and had the Spanish moss brush against your face like the hand of a wraith as it hangs from the live oak trees; if you've never ridden the streetcar in sticky summer heat so oppressive you could suffocate from its thick wetness; if you've never smelled the acrid burning scent of the leaves of the camphor trees that litter St. Charles Avenue, small and coppery like thin paper pennies; then you have nothing to miss, nothing to long for, nothing to mourn.

But I knew New Orleans before Katrina—I knew all those places and sounds and scents. I did dance till it was sunrise and did wander home in fogs thicker than any London had to offer. I was captivated by the city's magic and I don't want to think of it gone, forever, because then no one else would know what I know, no other young girl with unfettered dreaminess could go there and find everything she ever needed to know about love and loss and palpable yearning.

•

THERE IS A SCENE IN *Easy Rider*, an acid trip that takes place in the cemeteries down near Storyville, the old orphanage where Louis Armstrong and other bastard sons of the city were raised. The scene is shot with a fish-eye lens in supersaturated color and the characters are weaving in and out along the graves, which are raised chest-high because if they weren't built above ground every time it stormed—which is a few months every year, like monsoon season—the bodies would float Downtown and stop somewhere on Canal Street, right at the place the streetcar line ends, over at Carondelet.

That scene is how I lived my life in New Orleans: in a state of hyperintensity, as if I were on acid and everything dizzyingly, throbbingly hyper-real. How I saw everything when I lived in New Orleans was how the audience saw that scene: supersaturated, intolerably vivid. Where that scene took place was so close to where I worked, on the border between Treme and Desire, down low in the city, in the Ninth Ward, just beyond where white folks never crossed the color line except for those of us Northern girls brought in from outside to try and make things right, never mind the rage, never mind the rightful resentment they had of us with our blonde hair and perky expectations.

I feel some of that resentment myself now, as I listen to everyone else's plans for what's to come, as I hear that people—mostly black people—trying to rebuild their homes down there in the flood plain, may not be allowed to stay if enough people don't come back, as if *home* is mutable.

New Orleans was a city of ghosts, always, but it was never a ghost town like it is now. It was never a town with curfews and lights-out. There was always a place to listen to music and have a drink and do a little dancing and flirt with some stranger of any gender. The nights in New Orleans may have been fraught with danger, but they were never dark, never lonely, never lacking a jazzy melody line.

•

MOST EVERYONE HAS AT LEAST one life-altering experience sometime. New Orleans was the most defining for me. It became the filter through which I see everything. It was in New Orleans that I saw everything I would ever need to see to know how life works—and doesn't. Good and bad, black and white, young and old, New Orleans was all of it. There were the mysteries of jazz funerals and snake-handlers and voodoo spilling from French Quarter doorways. New Orleans was hot and gritty and full of often indecipherable smells. Insect-ridden and swampy. Loud and raucous, fog-muffled and eerie. Poverty-stricken and old-Southern-money elegant. It was all there—a discrete cross-section of American society with a decidedly foreign flavor. I was hungry for what it had and I ate it all up, let it drip from my lips, let it permeate me until I reeked of it.

•

I NEVER FOUND OUT IF there had ever been a streetcar named Desire and now I don't care to know. Desire is a place to walk through, the little whitewashed shotgun houses stacked side by side, scrubby grass and the errant banana plant stuck between the narrow buildings, a smattering of bougainvillea here and there to add some color. Dogs bark and children scream and shout and dark women with their hair covered in this or that fabric stand with their hands on their hips and look hard at you as you walk by but never say anything mean, never question your right to be walking there as if you belonged, because everyone's a stranger in New Orleans except the rich who own the place.

Smells come out of the houses—dirty rice and black-eyed peas, ham hocks mixed with greasy greens and red beans. This is Desire, this what I remember, this is what I still long for, this is *desire*.

No one would want to rebuild that, they say, because it's not middle class, it's not comfortable, it's not productive. It's just people living, hardscrabble, and barely getting by. Angry people who don't read too well and don't make much money and whose children might just grow up to be criminals instead of lawyers. Or at least that's what they say Uptown.

But here's the thing: Desire is New Orleans as much as the million-dollar-plus properties in the French Quarter and the Garden District. Black New Orleanians are as essential to the café-au-lait city as the rich white Uptowners. The little oil-can barbeque down in the Ninth Ward thick with ribs and crawdads is more New Orleans than the austere mesquite grills Uptown with their makis and tuna steaks. To have New Orleans, you have to have both— you must have both. Because otherwise you just have a tidy little white-on-white suburb with a Frenchified theme park in the Vieux Carré.

No one will learn anything from that. No one will stumble out into the fog and be surprised by the ghostly beauty of the night. No one will venture where they shouldn't go because there won't be anyplace where one shouldn't go. Sure there will still be music, but it will be Bourbon Street tourist music, not funky jazz, not music that spills out of the corner bar or the little eatery or the po'boy place. Everything will be tamed and toned down and muffled not by fog but by someone else's sense of what the place *should* be, now that we can start over, *fresh*.

•

KATRINA WAS A TRUE TRAGEDY, a life-altering disaster which, six months later as I write this, continues its destruction.

But here it is: Tragedy can be overcome. We don't have to remain broken forever. Memory can sustain us through the worst of times. My memories of New Orleans are warm and sweet as any Hummingbird biscuit drizzled in honey. My desire for those tiny, perpetually damp streets, to be lost in the thickest fog and come out of the mist to find something magical—all of that remains with me.

I want it back. I am not alone in that desire.

Most things go extinct because we are careless—we don't pay attention to the slow dwindling down and suddenly: gone. Forever.

Some of New Orleans is remarkably unshattered: the French Quarter, the Garden District. But other places—Desire, Treme— are decimated, many of those who lived there either dead or displaced and the Irish Channel is more channel than anything else now, rutted by Katrina and the Mississippi a few blocks over.

Yet in my memory all these places are still as they were— thriving, intense, throbbing with life.

I want that New Orleans back and whether or not you've ever been there, you should want it back as well. Because although we can hold things close to our hearts in memory, it is better to be able to renew that memory over and over by being *there*.

My lover has never been to New Orleans. I want to take her there—to show her this object of my lifelong desire. And so in my dreams we are there, standing in a thick pile of camphor leaves outside the Columns Hotel where I lived on the top floor in a tiny room with a bed, a sink and a desk and where the heat would suffuse the room and the cat who lived next door would run across the roof and come in through my window at dawn and nestle next to me on my bed. In my dreams we are listening to the Radiators way down in the Quarter and dancing until the sky is pink outside. In my dreams we are walking through Audubon Park and pulling down pieces of Spanish moss, twirling them in our fingers. In my dreams we are in Storyville, walking down Ramparts, hearing the far distant carillon of Saint Louis Cathedral. In my dreams New Orleans is the way it was. Whole and rich and full of every kind of life. In my dreams the scent of sweet olive is everywhere and Desire is real again, forever.

the upstairs lounge fire

pastor dexter brecht

JUNE 24, 1973, IS A date seared into the hearts of the LGBTQ citizens of New Orleans—literally, for thirty-two of them. While the burgeoning Gay Rights movement was causing celebrations to be held in other major cities around the U.S. that day, it was life as usual in New Orleans. The cultural priorities of the Big Easy were, and still are, good food and a good time. No one seemed to want to make too big of a commotion in the sweltering summer heat; so the usuals, along with a few visitors, gathered for the Upstairs Lounge's regular Sunday Afternoon beer bust.

"The usuals" were an eclectic mix of folks that included a dentist, pianist, linguist, federal employee, and radio engineer, as well as a mother who accompanied her two sons, and members of the Metropolitan Community Church who used the bash as their social hour following worship services. Alcohol was considered a staple of the diet and the special prices led to levels of consumption that resulted in the perception of a good time for all. The only apparent glitch in the good time on this particular afternoon was when someone was caught sneaking nearly emptied mugs away from the imbibers in order to turn them in and collect the deposit they were obtained with. The sneak thief was thrown out of the bar and the revelry continued—but the party ended in anything but the regular way just before 8:00 P.M.

Because the bar was located on the second floor, a special doorbell had been installed to signal the arrival of taxis. When the bell rang that night, the bartender knew he had not called a cab for anyone, so he decided to yell down the stairway to let the driver know. He pulled open the door to discover that the stairwell was an inferno. Whoever had rung the bell had apparently thrown a "Molotov cocktail" and then run. The back draft caused by the opening of the door filled the space above the suspended ceiling in the bar with fire. Within minutes the entire room was engulfed and confusion reigned.

Discovering the stairwell impassable, clients ran to the windows, only to find that they had been fitted with cast iron burglar bars. One patron did manage to squeeze through the bars, only to fall to his death. Another, the pastoral leader of the church, became wedged in the bars, and the crowd that had gathered below watched as the fire consumed him. Most of those gathered perished inside the place they had come to know as sanctuary. A handful of people did manage to escape when bartender Buddy Rasmussen led them through an unused backroom to a door that opened on to the roof of the building next door and through the window of an apartment in the next building. The fire department did respond quickly and had the fire under control in a reasonable amount of time, but it was not quick enough to prevent it from being the worst fire, in terms of human fatality, to have ever occurred in New Orleans.

Local reaction to the fire varied greatly. In contrast to the professional attitude of the New Orleans Fire Department, the Police Superintendent dismissed the tragedy of the situation in remarks to the local newspaper by discounting the bar as a place that petty thieves and homosexuals hung out. This sort of attitude might account for why the charred remains of the pastor were left on display in the window while the initial investigation was being conducted. New Orleans is also known as "The City That Care Forgot." That, combined with the blatant homophobic attitude of the police department, might explain in some measure why there were four bodies that were never claimed by next of kin and why the city of New Orleans refused to release them to the MCC, which had volunteered to bury them with dignity. There are LGBTQ people who were present in the city at the time of the fire who have now reported that they were either too afraid or too overwhelmed to publicly acknowledge their sense of grief and loss then. Perhaps this is why there was no locally organized LGBTQ response at that time. Fortunately, there were a few brave souls who stepped forward to do what was right. The Reverend William Richardson, rector of St. George's Episcopal Church, risked his position as pastor of that church by insisting that their chapel be made available for the first memorial service for those who perished.

The tragedy was horrific enough that it did garner the attention of and prompt a response from the emerging national leaders of the LGBTQ rights movement in the U.S. The Reverend Elder Troy D. Perry, founder of the Universal Fellowship of Metropolitan Community Churches, rushed to the city to insure that the surviving members of the local MCC were cared for, and that members of the LGBTQ community were respected during the investigating and reporting of the event. Reverend Perry joined with other national activists to arrange for a community-wide memorial service at St. Mark's United Methodist Church. The sanctuary was filled with LGBTQ citizens of New Orleans seeking solace and their allies expressing support. The service ended with the assembled joining hands and singing "United We Stand"—the same song that had often been sung at closing time at the Upstairs. The press gathered outside the church. Knowing the contextual concerns of those gathered, the Reverend Perry offered the opportunity to anyone who did not want be photographed or interviewed to leave the sanctuary by a side door. Not one mourner chose the side door option, and the fundamentalist preacher who had waited outside to condemn those present was overwhelmed by the newly united community.

Things change slowly in New Orleans, very slowly. One arrest was made during the investigation into the fire but the charges were subsequently dropped when it became evident that the person was actually in California at the time of the fire. The case has never been solved. Following the departure of the activists and the closing of the investigation, things tended to go back to pretty much the way they had been prior to the fire for LGBTQ people. Most seemed comfortable assuming what would later be known as a "don't ask, don't tell" policy regarding their sexual identity. Resentment was expressed by some queer folk that the activists had swooped into the city, stirred things up, taken a collection, and then left them to deal with the repercussions. The resentment continues to this day in some portions of the community. But not long after the fire, the first self-identified "gay" publication began to be circulated in places that LGBTQ people frequented. Because the funds collected at the memorial were to be used for burial expenses of the unclaimed victims, but the city prevented the remains from being released, that money was given to the publishers of the *Advocate* to be dispersed to other LGBTQ communities in need around the country. The activists' use of the media and organization of the memorial service demonstrated for those who were interested in forming an out and proud community that they could deliver their message to the community-at-large, organization was possible, and there was strength to be gained from uniting.

Twenty-five years after the fire, lesbian newspaper columnist and community activist Toni Pizanie and MCC of Greater New Orleans's Pastor Dexter Brecht united to coordinate a communitywide recognition of the Upstairs Fire. This time the gathering included representatives from several LGBTQ-affirming faith communities and the city councilman who represented the district in which the fire occurred, as well as a special guest, the Reverend. Troy Perry. Almost twice as many people gathered for this event as gathered for the first memorial service. The service concluded with participants led in traditional jazz-funeral style through the streets of New Orleans to the site of the fire, escorted by officers from the New Orleans Police Department. A fund was established to assist with the production and placement of a plaque commemorating the fire.

On the thirtieth anniversary of the fire, a group of New Orleans LGBTQ leaders coordinated the laying of a plaque at what was the entrance to the Upstairs Lounge on Iberville Street just off of Chartres. The installation was made with the full cooperation of the city. The Reverend Perry led a celebration service and joined representatives of various LGBTQ-based organizations in dedicating the plaque. A luncheon co-sponsored by the Mayor's Advisory Committee on LGBTQ issues followed the dedication. The featured speaker was former New Orleans fire superintendent William McCrossen, the man in charge of the department at the time of the fire, who apologized for any misconduct on the part of other city officials at the time of the fire. The plaque includes the names of those whose death gave life to the LGBTQ movement in New Orleans:

Ferris LeBlanc, Joe Bailey, Clarence McCloskey, Robert Lumpkin, Duane Mitchell, Louis Broussard, Dick Green, Kenneth Harrington, Willie Inez Warren, Eddie Warren, James Warren, William Larson, Perry Waters Jr., Gerald Gordon, John Golding Sr., Donald Dunbar, Luther Boggs, Adam Fontenot, Gary Anderson, David Gary, Herbert Cooley, Joseph Adams, Skip Getchell, James Hombrick, Reginald Adams Jr., Larry Stratton, George Matyi, Leon Maples, Douglas Williams, Unknown, Unknown, Unknown

coming out 101:
final exam

steve berman

Please take your seats. Remember to leave a space between you and the nearest student. You have two hours to complete the final exam.

•

I CAME TO NEW ORLEANS patently dull at eighteen. In high school, my friends had all been geeks. Straight ones too, as I was deeply in the closet, so deep they all assumed me asexual. Most had never had a girlfriend or been to a bash. I myself had never had a drink (other than a few sips of fortified wine at Passover), never watched a porn video, never been out on a date or kissed a girl or guy. I had never done anything the least bit sexual with another person.

I remember my folks walking me around the French Quarter and down Bourbon Street past the strip joints with their bold billboards, complete with photographs, my face bright red. Not that I was really prudish, but my folks were right there, after all. Plus, I really had no clue how to react to anything sexual, of any sort.

•

Coming Out 101: Final Exam
Identification: In a brief, two- to three-paragraph response,
identify the following persons or terms relating to the class readings
(worth 15 points)

1. *Michael Carte*
2. *Codependent relationship*
3. *Zeta Psi*

•

NOTHING PREPARED ME FOR LIFE on my own as a freshman. Having a crush on the biology teaching assistant (a girl) led me to the best and worst relationship in my life to date. No, not with her, but with Michael Carte, a drop-dead-gorgeous Italian from Columbus, Ohio. Five feet 10 inches tall and 180 pounds with muscles all over. He lived down the hall from my sliver-thin 110-pound self. I would never have dared spoken a word to him had he not spoken first to me the day after my first party.

My shy self was drawn to his charisma. My spending time with him began on the half-lie that I wanted advice on how to ask out the T.A. Soon, I cut classes so I could spend more time with him, including the precious moments when he'd shut the door and begin changing in front of me and me alone. I will never forget the sight of him naked.

Unfortunately, he quickly became an unhealthy obsession of mine. Or maybe it was deeper; a small part of me is still convinced that it was love, however one-sided. Whenever Mike dated, I was thrown into deep bouts of depression and jealousy.

Looking back, I should never have roomed with him. From sophomore to senior year, we lived together. I spent so many sleepless nights waiting for him to come back to the apartment from a party or a date. I cooked his meals, did his laundry, kept house. I craved even the slightest bit of attention, nearly swooned when he hugged me, even felt satisfied when he beat me that at least, even with the pain, came his notice of my presence.

I joined a fraternity because he was a member. What a bunch of idiots. I had nothing in common with any of them. The fraternity house was a shambles that stayed together more because of encrusted gelatin shots than nails or mortar.

I never had my photograph taken with them. I wonder even if they have any records of my being a brother. They punished my distance by refusing to let me mentor a pledge.

No one respected them on campus and they always had the fewest pledges during my time at Tulane. Mike deactivated and soon caused a scandal when he wanted to pledge another fraternity, one more infamous. I defended his actions to the others. By senior year, I left them.

•

Problem Solving: One of the important themes we covered this semester was responding to situations that test resolve and self-actualization. Consider the following situations and develop a detailed response to each (worth 25 points).

1. *You are at the back of a newsstand and reading a gay adult magazine. An older man standing nearby doing the same is looking up often from the pages to glance at you. Do you a) ignore him and*

*keep reading; b) seek to capture his attention more by stepping closer;
or c) glance back at him now and then but remain put?*

2. *The older man, who you found quite handsome, has put down the
   magazine he has been reading and leaves the newsstand without
   so much as saying a word to you. Do you a) shrug off his obvious
   disinterest; b) admit that you could not attract someone good-looking
   and sulk off; or c) quickly follow after him in a stalkerish manner?*

3. *The older man has seen you tailing him and has headed for a public
   bathroom. You follow him inside and see him enter a stall. Do you
   a) press on the stall door until he lets you inside; b) putter about the
   bathroom and wait for him to come out; or c) decide that anyplace
   that smells of urine is not a good site to lose your virginity and so
   leave?*

•

I REALLY HAD NO SOCIAL life at school and ate many of my
meals alone. I didn't date either. No one was interested. Well, the
only ones I asked out were a couple of girls in my classes. Their
responses ranged from mockery to sad shakes of the head. The
thought of being with a guy remained a delusion. The closest I
came was spending my parent's money on a few porn mags from
this little French Quarter newsstand not far from the farmer's
market.

I came close to losing my virginity one afternoon. A man in his
thirties or forties, dashing, with salt-and-pepper hair, and wearing
a business suit, must have decided to spend some of his lunch break
checking out the magazines. Then he started checking me out. I
didn't really believe it at the start—no one had ever thought me
the least bit attractive before then.

I followed him out and through the streets until he arrived at
the restroom. I never went into the stall. The idea that guys would

have sex in a bathroom never occurred to me. I waited outside but he never came out. I left feeling rejected; I had utterly misread him and was foolish and embarrassed to think someone like him would ever be interested in a kid like me. The crowded streetcar ride back to the apartment and Mike felt oppressive that day, like a prison routine.

•

Essay Question (chose from one of the below and write a minimum of four pages, worth 60 points):

While all "coming out" experiences are different, how does losing virginity stand in the chronology of accepting queer identity? Does the sexual act have to be homosexual in nature? OR

•

LOOKING BACK, I REMEMBER DESPERATELY wanting to date someone. I saw college friends dating and sleeping around and I wanted more of the former than the latter. Mostly, I did not know what to expect from sex, so dating was relatively safer—yet just as unobtainable, because during all my years at Tulane I never once successfully asked anyone out on a date.

I had turned twenty years old a couple of months before junior year. That October I was visiting the campus Winn-Dixie, a convenience store, and looking at the cheap mass-market books, when in walked this guy wearing Lycra all over. Mirrored sunglasses reflected my staring at his lithe body.

Without knowing that I was adopting the right method, we cruised with constant back-and-forth stolen glances. Finally, I walked out of the store. Walked reaaaal slow. I heard him behind me, with his bike in tow, and I instantly became thrilled when he caught up to me and began talking with me.

I soon realized he was gay and it became apparent that Juan (formerly of Puerto Rico but now living for several years in New Orleans) would like me to follow him back, through Audubon Park, to his little bungalow apartment. I did so, trying hard not to say the wrong thing and chase him away.

Desperation makes one do the most foolish things. Such as allow a roommate to slap you around. Or ignore the gigantic plaster phallic totems around a guy's apartment. Well, I couldn't really ignore them, but I didn't ask Juan about them either. They should have been my first warning that something was amiss.

Warning number two came when he began shedding. First his glasses, then his shirt. His face looked lined and tired and far older than I expected. His lithe body became scrawny, his skin at the shoulders scaly and raw-looking. Whatever attraction I felt for him began to dissipate fast. But I was trapped. I could not leave, could not abandon the first gay man I had ever talked to who wanted me.

We kissed. No romantic clichés. It felt perfunctory. We both stripped down. I tried to avoid looking in the mirrored closet door by the bed; neither of our bodies looked sexy—more starved. When he went down on me I felt nothing except a slight wetness and friction. Where were the great sensations, all the pleasure I had read about in the sordid little stories in those magazines? Why did the men moan so little? I had little passion while returning the favor.

He seemed content to simply masturbate. I did not like the look of his long nails so close to my dick. I begged to fuck. I wanted to experience everything (well, everything I knew of at the time) about gay sex. Not out of desire, but need. There had to be an explanation, a reason why everyone wanted to get laid. Otherwise . . . I didn't dare think of any otherwise.

Juan didn't want to fuck, though, until my begging finally cajoled him. He tried topping me, but it hurt so much that after a few strokes I demanded, screamed, for him to get out of me. Then he wanted me to top him. The act felt so mechanical, without the least pleasing sensation, that I soon had to stop. That and I caught a glimpse of myself in that mirror and I felt disgusted at what I saw.

He jerked off and came. I never did. Only when I scrambled my clothes back on did I realize the awful truth: We had played around without condoms. I asked him if I had any reason to worry. He said no.

When I came back to my apartment I took a long shower. The hot water eventually ran out and still I scraped and soaped my skin, wanting to get clean.

•

Are there stages of "coming out" as a rite of passage? If so, what are these stages and what social and sexual interactions can be expected in each?

•

I DIDN'T HAVE SEX AGAIN while at Tulane. Sex had betrayed me, lied to me. Oh, I still masturbated, but mostly to thoughts of what Mike did with the girls he brought home.

After graduation, I returned to New Jersey, but New Orleans rarely left my thoughts. Too much had happened. I had changed. The city had shepherded my evolution. When I wrote, nearly all my stories were either set in the Crescent City or involved some element of what I had witnessed there.

I did recover sexually. Sort of. In my mid- and late twenties I went through the Slut Phase a lot of gay men experience. But I rarely ever came with any of the one-night stands or short-lived dates I found. The pleasures rarely lasted and never crescendoed.

Years later, I returned to New Orleans to celebrate New Year's with friends. The city barely recognized me, yet made me feel welcome, as it never had when I was a scared teen. I was no longer in the closet with these friends but proud of being gay. I seemed to attract men too—from a sexy stripper at a bar who trapped my hand in his crotch for almost an hour, to the Asian student who agreed to rush off to a tryst and nearly strangled me because of his anti-Semitic feelings, though he still blew me. I had sex on a crowded dance floor while the minutes fell away from the old year.

But now, the old fears have returned. How long has it been since I felt a guy eye me? When was the last time I went out on a date? Been held in a tight embrace? Felt real pleasure from another's kiss and touch? Far too many years. I have let failures eat away at any confidence I once felt, until I am a shadow of my former self. Or a mirror image of a much, much former Steve.

Perhaps a cure can be found in an ancient neighborhood, filled with the sounds of laughter and jazz, the smells of fine and fast restaurants, the sights of iron balconies and decadent bodies. Or maybe a walk Uptown, past buildings where I once studied dead poets and writers. New Orleans. Such a fickle, such a wonderful muse.

I wonder how she will test me next time.

master eddie delis

martin pousson

Said she was coming, they did. Said it
before, how many times? Same fools who
promised him wine, promised him salad,

a golden haze he could chase to a new
car, new house, better living and better
days he never saw. Except through glass.

Said she was coming, the big one
this time. Wasn't gonna miss it, no sir.
Sat tight 'til she passed. All that howling

wind and thunder, all that flashing light
and rain. Wait, he waited for the storm
to stop, for the city to clear, the big glass

windows to bust open, then he stuck
his hand inside, grabbed it, all that flash
and bling, all that glitter and pomp

Rolex for him, another for his wife, hell
three, four Gucci bags too, Widescreen TV
stared at him too long, just took it from

thieves, all those CEOs and SOBs
who stole his dried-up raisin of a dream,
stole his son's horn, his daughter's song

his granddaddy's name. Just took a few beads
back. Circled it all like wagons in the den,
made his wife's blue eyes beam, she gave

him wine, gave him head too, like the golden
days they promised. Couldn't turn his loot on,
he didn't care, power comes back, still his

until the waters began to rise, the stink
and rot too. Everything floated away,
all his booty and kill. Found his body

in the river used to be the street. Parts
here and there, leg in a kitchen cabinet,
arm in a Golden Retriever's mouth.

Said all those parts were him, they did.
Found the TV on the stove, the bags
on someone else's roof, still searching

for his wife's body, the gold he missed.

shirley delis

martin pousson

Skinny man like him, big woman like her,
he never even saw her skin, though it
thrilled her. His coffee, her cream. "Stir it up,

little darling, stir it up," like atomic
gumbo. Skinny, yes, but she found the only
muscle that mattered. Their *au lait*

kids grew up with creole tongues
little octoroons, quadroons, still black
on the forms, in people's eyes, under

the law. Wanted for crimes they didn't
commit 'til it no longer mattered if they did.
One blew the cornet like nobody's

business, my Lil' Satchmo. 4th of July,
his horn blew bullets. Like all those kids
in Storyville, he'd learned to make music

from mud: bottle caps for checkers, salt rock
for diamonds, gun shots for fireworks.
But when his bullet pierced the sky, he got

rained down by the law. Fifteen, he was.
One year more than his sister, Lahalia
voice like an unsatisfied woman,

a cry unheard, she sang from the streets,
garbled verbs like her daddy, danced with taps
on her feet, daughter of Amos & Andy.

Brought supper home more than once, syphilis
too. Blew men for a Lincoln, sometimes
in a Lincoln. Heard boys down the block ask,

what did she charge for a screw? Got run out
of school, didn't feed her anyway.
Headed to the no-book red-lit classrooms

of the 9th Ward, the Him-N-Her club
the Dew Drop Inn. Only her degree
was terminal. Shot by a john in the

head; she'd refused to swallow. Big like
her mama was and bloated, just a grounded
barge, a Mardi Gras float, she couldn't

stop the bullets. Couldn't stop the storm
either. By the time the wind and rain came,
Shirley D had already evacuated

given it all away. Brick for cinder block, suburb
for projects, white for black, both kids. See
they were ready, Master Eddie and her.

Beads were doled out, doubloons too. Nest
emptied so come the storm they could float out
like two flightless birds, like a couple

of blank boats on a toxic swamp, a dead sea.

caring for the city
that care forgot

brian sands

MAYBE I WAS ASKING, OR expecting, too much?

Perhaps I had forgotten that one of the reasons I left my hometown of New York for New Orleans seventeen years earlier was that I was fed up with being in a city that only concerned itself with the biggest, newest, richest, fastest, sickest, latest, worst, most difficult, most challenging, hardest working, most terrible, most up-to-the-minute, most over-the-top. "More" simply isn't good enough. It's always gotta be the "most."

I had never evacuated before. Not for Andrew. Not for Georges. Not for Ivan. The Saturday before Katrina arrived I was Uptown marching along with hundreds of others as part of the nineteenth annual Krewe of OAK Midsummer Mardi Gras parade. Troy "Trombone Shorty" Andrews led. The Rebirth Brass Band played.

There was a flame breather. There were fireworks. Hurricane? What hurricane?

Eleven hours later, all that had changed. I awoke on Sunday to discover that, unlike previous storms that had had the courtesy to make a jog to the east or west before things got too hairy, this Category 5 monster was heading right at us.

A few phone calls and five-and-a-half hours later I was heading out of New Orleans with friends to Montgomery, Alabama. A friend, neighbor, and part-time French Quarter resident had opened up her family's beautiful home to a total of five of us, who ultimately converged on her house around 4:00 Monday morning.

Despite dealing with challenges of their own, including a daughter whose Mississippi boarding school had lost power and an elderly mother-in-law who had evacuated from Bay St. Louis to similarly powerless Hattiesburg, Emelyn and her family were ineffably kind, helpful, understanding, and accommodating; in short, extending the fabled Southern hospitality, including organizing a Tuesday night barbecue for friends, family, and we evacuees, at a time when the simple offer of temporary shelter would have been welcome enough.

After the levees broke and the city flooded and it became clear that no one was going back home anytime soon, I made arrangements to head up to New York. A round-trip special that was less expensive than any of the one-way flights I could find necessitated a ten day stay in Atlanta. Despite the gas crisis that had erupted, Emelyn was nice enough to drive me, carless and driving-challenged typical native New Yorker that I am, to LaGrange, Georgia, where a college friend met me at the mall. After a necessary visit to the J.C. Penney to augment the few T-shirts and shorts I had brought with me, we continued on to Atlanta.

Atlanta was incredibly welcoming. All the gay bars I went to seemed to be doing benefits or collecting money or dedicating some portion of their entrance fee to hurricane relief of one sort or another. Party promoter RC Searfoss, who had been planning to come to Southern Decadence, instead managed in three days to put together a late-night fundraiser dance at the Abbey that attracted more than 250 people.

My most special memory of my Katrina time in Atlanta is from when I went with my friend Floyd to the OK Café for a late afternoon bite to eat. Floyd, a political activist, frequent visitor to N'Awlins, and never one to be shy, let our waitress Sue know that I was an evacuee (or was it "refugee" that day? or "victim"?). Still recovering from all the food we had eaten at the jambalaya/gumbo party we had thrown the night before for about fifty friends and fellow evacuees, we split a Brunswick Stew (think of gumbo with chicken and corn off the cob rather than andouille and okra) and a sandwich. When we asked for the check, Sue, a willowy, athletic blond of a certain age, said, "This is on me," nodding in my direction. We tried to argue, Floyd chiming in, "He's not hurting" (by then, I was pretty sure that my apartment had emerged basically unscathed), but she wouldn't take any money. Needless to say we left a generous tip. I did make it clear to Floyd after we left the restaurant that, though my material losses may be few, I, like all other New Orleanians, was hurting on the inside.

When I arrived in New York on September 10, I soon discovered a city different from the one I had been in just ten months previously. It was as though it was September 10, 2001, all over again with all the civility that 9/11 had engendered now evaporated. In the ensuing weeks, I would find that NYC had completely regained its horn-honking, overcrowded sidewalk pushing, rush rush, don't-fuck-with-me mentality. If on one hand it seemed like the tragic wound had finally healed (a good indication that New Orleans's might do the same eventually), on the other, I kind of missed a certain gentility that had appeared to have taken root in Manhattan.

This did not fully sink in for a few weeks, however. My first days were spent in reactive mode—going to the Red Cross, obtaining an EBT card (food stamps, as it was once called), signing up for unemployment, and endless waiting to get through to FEMA on the phone. If my experiences were fairly benign, I empathized with those people who were far worse off than I was and did not have the social network of friends and family that I enjoyed in my hometown.

Still, there were bank accounts to be opened, as my New Orleans bank does not have any branches in the Northeast; try explaining to an uncomprehending bank manager that you don't have any ID with a local address because you have temporarily evacuated in the wake of Hurricane Katrina—or didn't she read the newspapers? There were the phone calls to every institution that might be sending me mail, giving them my new address, and the trips to the post office to see when the forwarding order I submitted in Atlanta would kick in, only to be told that any mail that wasn't flooded was likely to be returned to the senders. And the complete frustration of having a cell phone that could make calls but rarely received them.

On the positive side were all the benefits that were organized throughout New York for hurricane relief.

SEPTEMBER 12—A benefit for the Southern Rep (I am their literary manager), at Opaline in the East Village, was put together by a fellow theater company, Rude Mechanicals.

SEPTEMBER 14—A huge outdoor benefit/silent auction was sponsored by Jacques-Imo's on the West Side, with music and lots and lots of food—even though it took standing in line forty-five minutes to get any! (The time went by quickly as I chatted with a lovely young lady and former New Orleanian, with whom I traded jambalaya recipes.)

SEPTEMBER 25—A star-filled benefit on Broadway was hosted by Liza Minnelli and Ben Vereen and featured New Orleans's own

Bryan Batt singing "Do You Know What It Means to Miss New Orleans?" The Gershwin Theater was packed to the rafters and dozens of celebrities participated.

SEPTEMBER 29—Allen Toussaint continued his series of concerts at Joe's Pub at the Public Theater benefiting New Orleans musicians. Despite having lost his home, he had not lost his sangfroid and looked as dapper as ever.

OCTOBER 2—Crudo on the Lower East Side hosted a wine-tasting to raise money for the service industry workers' benefit fund. Four other restaurants on Clinton Street, including WD40 and Falai, contributed wonderful hors d'oeuvres.

OCTOBER 9—Local jazz vocalist Esquizito, displaced to NYC (I had met up with him at the Red Cross), participated in "Echoes of Katrina: Stories of Courage," a program of readings and music at the Ninth Avenue Saloon, with 100 percent of the donations going to Direct Relief International/St. John Humane Society to help evacuees and displaced animals.

OCTOBER 11—A benefit and silent auction took place at the midtown Cornell Club for the New Orleans Metropolitan Convention and Visitors Bureau's New Orleans Tourism Rebirth Fund. Joining three chefs from Manhattan were six who flew up from Louisiana just to participate in this event, representing such restaurants as LaCôte Brasserie, Dakota, and René Bistrot.

OCTOBER 16—HeartSong, a three hour extravaganza, featured stars of the cabaret world, from Kitty Carlisle Hart to Baby Jane Holzer to Julie Wilson. The evening at Symphony Space on the Upper West Side helped to jumpstart the CAC Performing Artists Fund.

OCTOBER 20—Will Clark's Porn Idol at the OW Bar on the East Side dedicated its finale to the NO/AIDS Task Force and raised $1,000 through a raffle and auction. Celebrity judges included Michael Musto of the *Village Voice*, promoter Bobby McGuire, female illusionist Charmaigne, porn star Manuel Torres, and yours truly. (Hey, being an evacuee has to have some benefits, y'know. Actually, I was delighted to be the one to connect Will Clark with Noel Twilbeck of the Task Force.

OCTOBER 24—A reading of *The Importance of Marrying Well$* plus silent auction at the Perry Street Theatre benefited Southern Rep. Dana Slamp, who wrote this witty updating of Oscar Wilde, wanted to do her part to help New Orleans; through networking she decided to help out New Orleans's only Equity theater and organized a delightful evening of entertainment, food, and drinks.

And these were just the events I was able to participate in. Of course there were also the ones that garnered major media attention, such as the pair featuring pop and rock stars at Madison Square Garden/Radio City Music Hall, and the one that Wynton Marsalis led at Lincoln Center.

Individuals helped out, too. The manager of a bicycle store gave me a break on a new lock. The casting director of the prestigious Manhattan Theatre Club, where *Proof* and *Doubt* originated, held open auditions for those actors from New Orleans displaced by Katrina. Afterward, she commented, "If the people I saw are any indication of the acting pool in New Orleans, there's a lot of talent down there."

And were it not for my friends who helped me out by letting me use their computers (my parents, with whom I was staying, only have the primitive WebTV), I would probably still be answering the countless e-mails I received in the storm's aftermath.

And yet.

And yet there were people who were so clueless. When I was having keys made in the Home Depot near Bloomingdale's a mere six weeks after the hurricane, a salesperson with a classic "bridge-and-tunnel" demeanor actually went off in my face about Governor Kathleen Blanco's not calling in the Federal Guard sooner. Who the fuck did he think he was? Never mind that not all the facts had come out yet; never mind the White House's campaign to smear the Democratic governor with lies and half truths and obfuscations about what she did or didn't do; and never mind that I doubt this blowhard could've done any better. I was not looking for a debate, nor did I want to be put in a position of having to defend my "peeps," when all I wanted was some new keys.

Still, overall, the response of New Yorkers was appropriate at first. Though I knew, even prior to my first trip back to New Orleans in mid-October, that my apartment was neither flooded nor looted, and was pretty sure it hadn't burned and its roof was okay, I was by no means certain. Most everyone I spoke to, with one notable exception (to be described below), exhibited concern and sympathy and wished me well.

But then talk would turn to other subjects and other problems and New Yorkers would complain about anything and everything as New Yorkers are wont to do. And, frankly, I wasn't interested. Not at all. It was as though I could see a mouth moving but whatever was coming out of it went right past my ears and evaporated into the ether. If I felt funny about this, as I talked to other New Orleanians I discovered they all felt the exact same way. Good news? Bring it on! Bad news? Everything non-Katrina could wait.

I returned from my first New Orleans visit on October 14, half happy to leave its surreal twilight zone, half wanting to stay and be part of the immediate recovery. My apartment was basically okay, other than one very moldy wall which I was able to clean up and a refrigerator that, despite cleaning, would eventually need to be replaced.

And as October turned into November turned into December

I was amazed at how New Yorkers' interest turned into apathy and indifference.

As the weather cooled, when I'd mention to someone that I was from New Orleans, always the first question was, "How's your house/home/apartment?" or "Did you get flooded?" with a look of concern edged with the gallows interest that occurs as motorists slow down when passing an accident. Of course, in NYC it's always all about the real estate. When others were told I had just one moldy wall and a nasty but now cleaned-up fridge, the concern and curiosity just drained from their faces—replaced in part with a soupçon of disappointment that they couldn't then go back to their offices, their boyfriends, the guys with whom they go bowling or to the opera, and say, "I met this guy from New Orleans who lost everything, EVERYTHING!"

In the one-upmanship game that is so the City, I was merely an opening gambit— "guy from NOLA with a moldy wall"—easily trumped by "guy from NOLA who was flooded," which in turn would be outdone by "guy from NOLA who lost everything," and then the ultimate ace, "guy from NOLA who wound up in the Superdome or Convention Center," which could fuel cocktail/ dinner-party talk for weeks if not months. I could envision how mouths would water if I could only provide details of seeing starving people or rapes or murders or dead bodies in the street. Now *that* would make their eyes light up.

It seemed as though Louisiana's response to 9/11 had been forgotten. I kept wanting to say, "Gumbo Krewe, Gumbo Krewe" to remind them of the incredible folks who went up there on their own dime to serve a delicious, homemade version of one of our signature local dishes to recovery workers at Ground Zero. Not to mention how New Orleans bought NYC a fire truck to help replace those crushed by the collapse of the World Trade Center.

And it wasn't like their attention was now consumed by Hurricane Rita or the earthquake in Pakistan. Those events barely merited a blip on their radar screens.

And it's not like they didn't know what was going on. *The New York Times*, unique among our nation's daily papers, provided superb ongoing front-page coverage from nearly every perspective. (That said, trying to get the *Times* to donate a single subscription of its august product to the financially strapped N.O. Public Library has proven to be a Herculean task.)

You who are reading this might wonder, "Was it just him? Or just the people he encountered?" No, it wasn't. As I was writing this, I spoke to a friend/acquaintance who was in New York in early December who experienced the same response. He even claimed he had people asking him, "Is everything okay there yet?" And this was just three months after the storm! I could recall visiting Manhattan in January 2002 when a deathly pall still hung over the borough four months after the terrorist attack. Why would anyone think things would be much different after the greatest natural disaster in United States history?

So perhaps after the incredible Southern hospitality of Emelyn in Montgomery and Sue at the OK Café and all I heard about people from Houston to Atlanta and all the small towns in between going out of their way to open up their homes and businesses and helping people out with meals and rides and haircuts and you name it, I was expecting more.

But after my first encounter following my arrival at LaGuardia Airport from Atlanta on September 10, maybe I should have expected nothing at all.

It was a beautiful day. The flight had been a smooth one. All I had with me was a stuffed backpack and an overnight bag that wasn't so stuffed.

I got on the public bus that would bring me into Manhattan. It was crowded. I took a seat in the back. I put the overnight bag underneath it, took a script out of the backpack, and then placed the backpack on the floor.

I opened the script. Immersed in it, I was barely aware that its cover was gently touching the leg of the man sitting next to me.

After ten minutes or so, he imperiously said to me, "Get that off of me."

I looked at him. He was an average looking guy in his mid- to late forties. Balding with glasses he had the look of a Mr. Potato Head come to life. He was overweight but not outrageously so, not by today's standards. But he was definitely squooshing me into the arm rest on the other side of my seat.

I responded in kind: "Get your leg to your side of the seat," as his plump thigh had gone beyond the demarcation line of the sitting positions.

Could I have accommodated him? Perhaps. Certainly if he had said "please." But I was in no mood for petty shenanigans less than two weeks after escaping from a hurricane. After all, what did I have to lose?

I shifted my position and removed the offending plastic cover from his delicate knee. A few minutes later, uncomfortable, I shifted back. The cover touched him again.

"Do as I told you to do," he bellowed. I'm not making this up. I looked at him again. My gaydar went off. He seemed to be a mid-level bureaucrat of some sort, perhaps in academia, used to giving orders, used to having them obeyed.

Next to him was sitting the man whom he had picked up at the airport. A gentle-seeming, mild-mannered type, he visibly cringed. A couple? No, more likely just friends. I couldn't imagine this pissy would-be Queen Bee being involved with anyone but himself.

With images of police, state troopers and other emergency personnel giving orders over the past twelve days, I did the only logical thing I could do. I laughed. And laughed and laughed. A good hearty belly laugh. I could feel the pressure, pressure I had almost been unaware of, being released.

The fat fag then said, "Are you finished having your nervous breakdown?"—words forever etched in my memory.

By now, everyone around us was watching this battle of wills.

"I just arrived here after evacuating from New Orleans," I

replied, "and if I want to have a nervous breakdown, I think I'm entitled to." Okay, maybe not the greatest response, but it was the best I could do under the circumstances. In any case it shut him up. I sensed his brain was straining for an appropriate comeback. I think I could even see his tongue trying to form words, but he wisely relented.

As we traveled through Queens, I returned to my reading. A few minutes later this overweight weasel narrowed his eyes and, with the middling intelligence of a third-rate private eye refusing to believe the obvious, questioned me with, "Are you really from New Orleans?"

"Yeah."

I waited for an apology. It never came from this miserable excuse for a human being. He eventually exited the bus, meek friend in tow, embarrassing himself, his city, homosexuals, men, in short, the human race.

Okay, perhaps I exaggerate. Now I can even laugh at that abominable piece of lumpen proletariat.

But at the time it left me shaken, unbelieving that anyone who lives in a city that had so recently endured what New York had gone through could be so insensitive, so callous and, when confronted, could remain so unrepentant. I wondered if he had known anyone who had perished in the World Trade towers and how he felt about it and how he expected others to feel. I wondered if he had ever known loss or if living in New York had inured him to such feelings. I wondered if he had ever had the experience of having his life poured into a blender, run at full speed, and then poured out. I don't know, but I think not.

But I'm not bitter at NYC. Saddened, maybe, but not bitter. Life does go on.

I read how NYC Loves NOLA, a "patriotic tourism initiative," recently brought nearly 200 members of New York officialdom to help New Orleans rebuild as a way of thanking those who traveled to the Big Apple to rebuild the city's economy and spirit after 9/11.

I'd like to think that, with the exception of my friend on the bus, everyone's heart is in the right place.

But should any average (or not-so-average) New Yawker be reading this, please keep this in mind: If Louisiana or any other place should go through a Katrina-like debacle again next hurricane season or the season after—if you meet any evacuees, even if they say they're okay, even if it's three or four or five months after the storm, just keep asking them questions about what they're going through, inquire about their friends and their friends' friends, and unless you have something really, REALLY big to complain about, save it for another time.

For if we were all New Yorkers after 9/11, Americans, New Yorkers included, should realize that we are all victims of Hurricane Katrina. There is a world west of the Hudson River and it remains there even after it may fade from the headlines.

two new orleans memories

timothy state

FOAM PARTY

IT WAS CHANCE'S BIRTHDAY. CHANCE keeps us young; the twentysomething amongst a crowd of thirtysomethings with two fortysomethings behaving like they were sixtysomething. Since it was his birthday, we all agreed to do what he wanted to do. We would spend a weekend in New Orleans, which is short for drink like a fish, and flirt with boys.

Early one afternoon, poolside at our bed and breakfast, we began negotiations for the evening's activities. It was a passive-aggressive game of manipulation spanning three or four tanning rotations at the clothing-optional pool. Trying to coordinate the agendas of six gay men is like landing a 747 without the user manual. One salivates for expensive, creative food, while another wants quick and easy. One prefers a bar with lots of pretty boys, but not too pretty so he can still compete, and another would like to be where the locals hang out, preferably with a few strippers to amuse the senses, and yet another dreams of a bar with dark corners where men lurk and grope but will die before admitting it. One wants to dance the night away, another wants to get drunk and make out with tourists.

Chance paged through the local gay rags, scanning the ads and calendars of events. He floated ideas for response.

"Cowpokes has lube wrestling."

"That sounds hot," I said; the thought of losing while wrestling a well-lubed Chance melted away the previous evening's hangover.

"No, we are not doing no lube wrestling."

"Would you enter?" I asked Chance.

"I said, *NO*. We are not lube wrestling and you are not entering. Besides, the place is called Cowpokes."

"How about going to Big Daddy's, daddy?" Daddy, despite behaving like it, is not the oldest amongst us, but he's fallen asleep in the lounge chair, an environmental awareness magazine leaving a rectangular tan line across his chest.

"Big Daddy's sounds skanky enough," I said. Being surrounded by big, burly, hairy men with dainty cocktail glasses in their man hands felt like innocent fun.

"I'm not hanging out with ugly people."

"But the ugly people are the most colorful," I said.

"None of this 'I wanna do what the locals do. Eat what the locals eat.' I want to go to a tourist trap where there are *attractive* people."

"I agree. Hell, I'm on vacation. If I wanna look at ugly people, I can do that any day at home."

"It's New Meat night at the Corner Pocket," Chance suggested.

"You could scratch a ball or two there." Of course, I was purely thinking of shooting pool.

"I'm much better with my cues and balls than you suggest." Chance glared at me with a tempting smile.

"NO! You are not entering no contest encouraging you to parade around half naked. You don't need that sort of reinforcement. Parading around here is plenty naked enough."

"If I don't get to flirt with at least one stripper, this trip will be a total waste," I said, making sure we set some standards.

"How could you say that?" Chance asked. "You're with me."

"So you're gonna shake it for me?"

Chance giggled his evil giggle.

"That's what I thought. We're *at least* stopping by Corner Pocket for *one drink*."

"Not until *after* the new meat contest."

"Looks like the only thing we can agree on is the Foam Party at Bourbon Street Pub," Chance said. He found out about the party a few days before leaving for New Orleans and instructed us all to bring appropriate clothing, including footwear that we wouldn't mind being destroyed. He went to Payless ShoeSource and bought all of us matching cheap slip-on shoes—his gift to us on his birthday, a souvenir of our time in New Orleans together, and insurance we'd have to go to the foam party.

"I'm not sold on this foam party concept. I think they're dangerous. I mean, can't you get an STD? A rash, or something you need a prescribed ointment to clear up?"

"I think that depends on who you touch. And if you can keep everything in your pants."

"I hear you can get pinkeye faster than if you chaperoned a field trip of fourth-graders."

"No you can't. It's no more dangerous than a bubble bath," Chance said.

Slipping and falling and getting a concussion, then continuing to dance the night away without knowing that one's brain is swelling is really the prime health risk of foam parties. At least that's all that came up when Chance Googled "Foam Party Health

Risk" on the poolside wireless at our Lower Garden District bed and breakfast. And since it was on the Internet, we all knew it had to be complete and accurate, similar to the bank transfer from Nigeria that will take place once we provide our bank routing and account number.

"No pinkeye. No sexually transmitted diseases," Chance said, lounging in the deck chair. Only a laptop covered his naked body. "No rare African bird virus known to eat away human skin will thrive in the foam of a dance floor. And besides, it's *my* birthday."

All of us except for Chance were skeptical, yet intrigued. He was playing up the seduction, which was his only purpose in lying naked. His sinewy body is beautiful. He knows it, and he knows we know it. More specifically, he knows I know it. Ever since that one drunken night that left him forever referring to me as "Sloppy Jalopy" because of one aggressively affectionate make-out session.

"How could you deny the opportunity to dance up against this?" he asked, his hand waving over his body as if it were the grand prize on the showcase showdown.

A minor concussion seemed like a small risk for the opportunity to roll around in foam mostly naked with Chance.

That's the purpose of a foam party; to dance as hot and sexy as one normally would with others, but with a frothing layer of foam added to the mix. Club-goers check their clothes to be wrapped in plastic grocery bags by the bar staff and then walk onto a dance floor of flashing strobes, colored gels, fog and disco balls. Two large machines on the ceiling churn out dollops of bubbles that drop onto the crowd below. A Plexiglas fence surrounds the area so the chemically generated foam can build up.

On posters hanging at eye level around the dance floor, the manufacturer of the foam machine assured us that dancing in foam was completely safe, although eye contact should be avoided. We were dancing at our own risk, they further pointed out. I suppose that's a general disclaimer seen almost anywhere; the roller coaster is absolutely safe. Until an axle breaks, and then who knows what might happen.

We were completely prepared. We all had our swimsuits, Velcro-tabbed pockets for cash, IDs, and whatever else we did not want to part with, as well as new pairs of six-dollar shoes from Payless ShoeSource that we could dispose of, if need be. We looked more like a group of balding high school teens heading to a water park than six gay boys out for a night of disco dancing.

A dozen dancers gyrated like Fisher-Price people bobbing around in a washing machine, only they were ugly, at least what I could see of them. If the warning signs had indicated chemical bloat a potential danger, I would have believed it, looking at these Michelin Tire Men. While I wanted to see skank, I didn't necessarily want to roll around with it in a foam bath.

Off to one side of the dance floor was a cocktail lounge with an Arabian Knight feel. Voluptuous velour and satin-covered pillows filled booths that were simply mattresses with curtains draped open. The lure of seductive temptation under the glow of Mediterranean chandeliers was overwhelming. A few beers into the evening, a corner Mediterranean escape and the light might just overpower Chance into a momentary Sloppy Jalopy session.

The odorless chemicals used for the foam gripped at our throats like chlorine gas at first, but we very quickly got used to the shallow breaths necessary to keep going. We ordered cocktails and scoped out the scene frothing before us. A beautiful buff boy, the picture of New Orleans I had hoped for, sat on the bar stool next to me. I could have easily dove into the dance floor with him. He wore a Speedo and had a pair of goggles on his forehead. Goggles. Why hadn't I thought of goggles?

Once we had a few cocktails in us, we checked our clothes and wandered into the shoulder-deep foam. Three of us came wearing swim trunks, prepared to only check our T-shirts. Chance came dressed for a production; to Chance there is no such thing as *un*dressing. He stripped his tight shirt from his torso as if peeling a banana, and rather than dropping his shorts, he slid them down his legs only after the waist got hung up as he bent over to emphasize the way his butt perfectly filled a seamless pair of white briefs. There is not enough fabric; even in public, Chance has figured out a way to leave nothing to my imagination while at the same time fueling nothing but my imagination. I am victim of both.

We dove into the dance floor.

It was like being in an ultimate full-body bubble bath. For a good hour, we waded through the foam, blowing bubbles and dancing up against each other. The foam created a slick, sexy, groping dance experience. A bubble bath made dirty. However, for every time I brushed up against Chance, there were multiple trolls diving amongst the foam, groping at our swim trunks, or the Michelin Tire Man spinning into us. It was like standing in the surf and having a large fish brush up against you, only worse—it's your grandpa amongst the foam.

It is difficult to breathe when overcome by a giant wall of foam. I'd try to wipe the foam from in front of my face, only to replace it with the foam clinging to my arm. At one point, the fog machine came on and very quickly we found ourselves dancing in a foam/fog whiteout. I understood what it would be like to be trapped in a nightclub fire. As I twirled in the fog, a wall of foam engulfed me. There was no freight train roar of a tidal wave or tornado. No Doppler radar or perky weatherman announcing the swell of a hurricane. Just the thumping disco beat of Sophie Ellis-Bextor's "Murder on the Dance Floor."

I turned in the general direction of an exit I could not see and clawed my way through the foam until I reached the Plexiglas containment wall. I clutched the rail and threw my upper body over it. Foaming at the mouth and trying to clear my airway, I coughed up chemical bubbles from my lungs and nose. In that moment, I was nowhere near as sexy as a "Baywatch" drowning victim. Still, I gloried. I had survived the wall of foam and fog and lived to tell about it. I was also quite certain that I had escaped a concussion.

The music transitioned to a Euro-pop dance remix of the Bee Gees' "Tragedy," and I took the track title as a divine message. It was time for a bubble break. I stood at the makeshift shower and washed the chemical bubbles from my body. We had been advised to slather baby oil over ourselves so the chemicals would wash off more easily. We had failed to comply, and in that one instant I wished I heeded the advice as great wisdom.

As I stood in the stream of water I opened my swim trunks to rinse off the foam that had found its way inside. And as the water washed the chemicals over and away from my manhood, I experienced a most intense shard of pain. I grabbed my genitals, winced in glorified agony, and jumped around like a toddler doing the potty dance. Mr. Bubbles these were not.

No one had warned us. Not the Internet, not the circuit boys lounging around the pool at our hotel, not even the signs. No one had mentioned anything about *chafing*. My god. The chafing. Dripping wet, clutching myself and with my shoes still filled with water, I ran to the restroom to examine the situation more closely. I dropped my shorts around my ankles and gently coddled my throbbing genitals. The tip, where my peter had rubbed up against the inside of my swim trunks, was red and swollen. It was seeping blood, like a very rare tube steak.

My evening, tragically, chafed to a close.

I dried off with a courtesy towel, emptied out my shoes, gently dabbed my sensitive self, carefully pulled my shorts up, and then went to sit at the bar, where I watched the foaming action from a distance. The Arabian booths were filled with boys and cocktails. The beauty factor rose with the foam on the dance floor, and I watched Chance gyrate into a whipped social frenzy of masculine goodness. I ordered a Kool-Aid shot from the bartender, hoping the sweetness would clear the chemicals clinging to the inside of my throat and at the same time numb my social and physical pain.

Chance threw himself against the Plexiglas, squishing his torso flat to the surface. He squirmed and shook his excited briefs to the beat of the music. Chance had no rhythm, but presenting a fishbowl view like that, he didn't need an orchestra to move to his own beat.

"Don't you want to dance with this?" he asked.

"Of course. But later."

"Okay. But if you love me, you'll buy me a beer," Chance said.

It was more comfortable to sit than to stand, so I moved my bar stool next to the dance floor and held Chance's Rolling Rock. Between each song, he came over so I could hand it to him.

"What's the matter?" he asked.

"I'm just taking a break."

"You not feeling well?"

If the highest concentration of nerve endings exists in the tip of the wee-wee, I had inadvertently found every single one of mine.

"You could say that."

"Oh." He looked concerned. "Travel constipation?"

"NO!"

"I'm just asking."

"The chemicals are getting to me."

A short time later, two more of our party showed up doing the chafed shuffle while Chance continued on the fermenting dance floor. It wasn't even 11:00. The dance floor had now filled with the hot, beautiful men Chance was hoping to flirt amongst, yet the pain on our faces told an unmistakable story. Amateur night was over. Chance agreed to forfeit his birthday evening and we made our way to the street.

"Shall we walk through the French Quarter?" he asked.

"I'd love to, if I could. You can, but I think I need to catch a cab." We hailed a cab and the healthy ones climbed into the back of the minivan, the maimed crawling into the front.

"I didn't even get to ogle a stripper," I mused, tears welling in my chemically stinging eyes.

When we got back to the bed and breakfast the three of us huddled in a circle and compared our injuries. All three, chafed beyond recognition.

While none of us are medical doctors, our amateur forensics investigation concluded that the injuries were located exactly where the rubber meets the road, where our masculine selves naturally rub up against our nylon swim trunks. The friction, combined with the chemicals in the foam, made for a disastrous combination. Our friends who got off chafe-free had all worn 100-percent natural cotton, in a supportive brief that coddled the genitals, holding them close and tight, in a nice basket of masculine goodness.

The more surface area one had, the worse the damage was.

We slipped into the bed and breakfast's hot tub. The warm water soothed our swollen and sensitive parts. Chance climbed in, his beautiful body unscathed. He sat next to me.

"Oh, not so close," I said, the pain making it difficult to move.

The chemicals that had produced the great wall of foam were still coming off our bodies and the hot tub began to froth. Mountains of foam formed in the center of the hot tub.

"Too bad," he said. "You *did* look pretty sexy tonight."

THE CREASE IN MY PALM

YOU HAVE A WAY WITH words," the Palm Reader said to me. "Mercury rules you."

He held my hand, running his fingers over the lines, cracks, and folds. He lightly dusted my palm with the tips of his fingers. It tickled. I flinched. Clasping our fingers together, he locked his eyes onto mine.

"The way you use words. You conduct them. Like an orchestra. And you bring people together with the music and the vivid pictures you create."

A tattered straw cowboy hat perched on his head. He wore a paisley and red silk shirt which drifted open as he moved, exposing a hairy chest and several gold chains with dragon pendants. A thick, heavy stubble covered his face, yet his voice was soft and calm.

He pulled on my hands, leading me to a chair, drawing me in. A card table sat in front of him, and two chairs on both sides of him had been wedged into the closed storefront alcove.

"Excuse me," I said to the woman next to him. "I didn't mean to interrupt your conversation."

She nodded her head in a circle, as if to signal that she understood not a word, but knew exactly what was going on.

"She's just my mother," the Palm Reader said. "She doesn't speak a word of English."

He looked more closely at my hands. He told me that success would come my way, if I were willing to receive it. He told me I form intense relationships. And he told me I was intuitive. Very intuitive, which would grow in strength over time. He pointed to the line indicating this, and said it would get deeper and longer the older I got.

"The challenge will be for you to accept that intuition. To accept it as real, which it will be." A voice in my head said he spoke the truth, but I did not want to believe it.

He held up his hand and pointed to the same line in his palm. It was distinct and deep, extending all the way across his hand. It even started to wrap around to the front.

"See, I'm very intuitive. It comes to me naturally." His hands looked like those of a wise old man—calloused and worn from a lifetime of hardship, yet he could have only been in his thirties, and certainly not older than forty.

"What are you doing tonight?" he asked, with a smile. It was cute, despite his teeth being crooked.

"I think I'm headed back to my bed and breakfast. Why?" It was a lie. I was visiting for a weekend of writing and relaxation and I had every intention of exploring New Orleans's reputation that precedes itself. Its pungent odors, gritty street scenes, and seductive boys lurking in dark corners lend themselves to behaviors normally relegated to one's imagination. While I had no idea what sinful temptations I was looking for, one tends to imagine the unimaginable when surrounded by decadent pleasures. The lines between reality and fantasy were quickly becoming a flirtatious blur as shamelessness was absorbed into the humid darkness, holding onto the unfolding secrets of my vacation.

"Well, I was thinking of going to the Voodoo Lounge for a cocktail when I'm done here. A friend works there. And I was thinking you might want to join me."

Lightly tickling the hair on the back of my hand, his fingers breezed perpetually over my hand. It was intoxicating.

"How long are you going to be here?" I asked.

"Not much longer. It's really slowed down. You have a nice glow. Your aura, it's very bright and positive." He had a way of ending every statement with an affirmation of how wonderful I was.

"What color am I?"

"Purple," he said without hesitation.

"Ah. The color of positive energy."

"You know what I'm talking about."

"A little."

"Can I call you?"

While I didn't anticipate seeing him again, an inner voice told me he would call; I could feel it in the crease of my hand. He reached for a cell phone in his pocket. I told him my number. He programmed it into his phone. I headed down the street into the early morning darkness of the French Quarter.

•

FORTY-FIVE MINUTES LATER, MY cell phone rang, displaying a number and an area code I did not recognize. I answered.

"Meet me at the Voodoo Lounge. I'd like to see you."

"Okay. I think I know where you're talking about. When you're standing in Jackson Square, do you go upstream or downstream?"

"Downriver."

"How soon will you be there?"

"As soon as I take my mother home. I'm almost there."

•

The Voodoo Lounge was not very far from Good Friends, the bar where I was talking with some locals. It also wasn't very far out of the way from my bed and breakfast. I went and sat at the bar, waiting behind my cocktail for the Palm Reader to join me. It was dark; voodoo dolls hung from the ceiling and on the knotty pine walls. Artwork celebrating the ritual adorned the walls. Despite the sinister ambience, I felt as if I was a regular. There were only three people in the bar; the bartender who was busy shutting the place down, and two people eating sandwiches with their cocktails.

The Palm Reader walked in the door and sat down on the bar stool next to me, straddling one of my legs. His teeth were crooked, but I found his smile absolutely captivating. He wasn't clean-shaven, but he had a neat look about him, that was just as striking as it was on the street. The perfection of beauty is found in flaws.

"I'm so glad you're here," he said.

"Where else would I be?"

"I don't know." Reaching for the side of my face, he smiled. He placed his hand behind my ear and gently rubbed. "I'm just glad you're here. I knew you'd be here."

"Intuition?"

"Yes. The voices."

He grabbed my hand. "I like your rings," he said, turning them around my fingers. "It's good you wear silver."

"Is it?"

"Silver protects you."

Even though I was not a quarter of the way through my Cape Cod, he ordered another for me and a drink for himself.

•

THE BAR WAS CLOSING. IT was getting late, I was full on alcohol, and I was talking with a palm reader who lived with his mother.

"I should go," I said with sobering authority. "Thank you for the drink." I got up to walk to the door, my heel catching on the bar stool, causing me to stumble. I walked away from one-and-a-half cocktails on the counter.

"Wait. Where are you going?"

"Back to my bed and breakfast," I said.

"Let me give you a ride at least."

"I can walk."

"I just don't want you to leave yet. I'd like to spend some time with you."

"I really must go."

He followed me.

We walked down the street to a silver Chrysler minivan that looked like it had been ridden hard. The windshield was cracked, the paint worn thin. His card table and chairs sat where car seats should have been. It was the picture of a van that mothers across the country have in their mind when they instruct their children to run in the other direction. Serial killers are generally the quiet type who live next door, blending silently into mainstream society. Certainly, they don't pose with their mothers as palm readers in the French Quarter. I climbed into the front seat.

Was I ignoring the crease in my palm? Or was I following it?

•

THE VAN WAS MUSTY FROM cigarette smoke. A voodoo doll hung from the rearview mirror. I cracked the window and turned my face toward the fresh air.

"I don't totally believe in the voodoo, I just think the doll is kind of cool."

"Just partially believe?"

He didn't answer. "I'm so sorry about the cigarette smell. I normally don't have guests in the car who care. You do care about the cigarette smoke, don't you? I can tell."

"It's okay. Thanks for the ride."

"My mother asked me what I was doing when I let you walk away." More than he watched the road, he watched me.

"Oh?"

"She wanted you to help us carry the card table to the car. You know she's eighty-three. She doesn't look eighty-three, does she?" He smiled at me. I wondered if she wanted him to stop me for a reason other than helping with the card table. "So why are you here in New Orleans?"

"I'm here for a writer's convention."

"I knew it. I knew you were a person of words. I hate that I'm right. I hate always being right." He shook his head. "It's a tremendous burden, you know."

The extreme world of New Orleans drifted by outside the window. Street people were settling down in doorways for the night. Drunken tourists stumbled back to their hotels. The neon of the night flashed. I was completely shielded from the grittiness of New Orleans, and at the same time completely enveloped in it.

"How could it be a burden?"

"Well, it's not so much any more. I've learned to tune out the voice. I've learned to ignore it when I want there to be intrigue. But still, it's hard. Do you have any of your writing with you?"

"Yes. In my room."

"Will you get it? Can I hear some?"

"Sure."

He parked the car, and followed me into the bed and breakfast. I invited him to sit down by the pool area. The other guests were in their rooms asleep; shortly the sun would bring a new day. I went to my room, returning with a folder of my writing. I sat next to him on the patio chair. The hot tub filter filled the air with static noise, our conversation cloaked in privacy. The landscape lights glowed blue, red, yellow, and orange, creating a tropical night scene.

"You're so beautiful in this light," he said.

"Thanks." I pulled a story out of my folder and as I read, he reached behind my knee, pulling my leg onto his lap. He stroked my leg lightly. He listened intently, releasing his hands to begin exploring my body as I read.

"That was really nice," he said when I had finished reading. I wondered if he spoke of my writing or running his hands across my body. He caressed my leg, his hand occasionally drifting up my shorts. "You have such a way of making words come alive. It's nice."

My skin came alive under his hands.

•

"I HAVE KIND OF A weird hobby," he said as his hand pressed hard on me.

"Weirder than reading palms?"

"Yeah."

I was captivated.

"I like to shoot photographs of people hanging from the ceiling in body bags."

I wondered what disturbed me more. Was it the fact he liked to photograph death? Was it the use of the word *shoot*? Was he suggesting that he would like to photograph me in a body bag? And when was the last time I'd heard a national Amber Alert for a missing gay white male? In a body bag? The crease in my hand was growing deeper.

What would the police say to my boyfriend back home? *We found him dead in a body bag, and we're not really sure what happened. But here are a few Polaroids.* I would be the stupid white guy in a

horror movie, walking into the hands of the crazed lunatic, drunk
on charm.

"Do you shoot film or digital?" I asked, ignoring the crease in
my hand.

"Digital. I shouldn't have told you this." He shook his head, his
face filling with regret. "I've told you too much."

•

"HAVE YOU EVER SEEN THE movie *Before Sunrise*?" he
asked.

"Hmmm. Sounds familiar. Who's in it?"

"Ethan Hawke. He meets a woman while traveling."

"Yes. I saw it last month, actually."

In *Before Sunrise*, Ethan Hawke encounters a woman on a train
and they connect in a moment. They spend the next fourteen
hours together, discovering an unrehearsed, unexpected, and
unexplainable love. The two characters face a decision, based on
their gut. Will they side with their feelings of the moment, risking
their lives to meet their soul mate? Is the feeling mutual? Can they
trust themselves? Each other? Or will they say goodbye, never to
see one another again?

•

"CAN I KISS YOU?" HE asked, sitting naked on the edge of
the hot tub. Chest hair swirled down his tight body to an arrow
pointing to his groin. He looked like a statue of wisdom. I was
already in the water.

I leaned toward him, his legs spread apart and he wrapped his
arms around me. Our lips engaged; I inhaled his earthy taste. As he
slipped into the water, I wrapped my arms around his body.

"I knew there was water in my evening," he said.

"Intuition?"

"I guess. I just knew there was water coming."

He licked my nipple, rubbing the stubble on his chin into it, making it erect. A tickle shot through my body, and exited through my groin. My body and pleasure his destination; his lips and intuition his guide.

•

"SO THIS IS IT," HE said. "This is goodbye." Still wet from the hot tub, his shirt soaked up his chest hair.

"Maybe we'll see each other again. Do you have e-mail?"

"No."

"Well, maybe tomorrow night?"

"I won't be working tomorrow. This is it. This is goodbye. I'm just another chapter in your book."

"Yes," I said. I unlocked the gate that separated the tranquility of the patio from the street loonies. He stepped out and turned to me. We kissed. Our hands clasped. Our fingers intertwined. The stubble on his face brushed against my lips one last time. He took a step backward. His body followed. Our fingers slid apart. He pivoted on his foot, and disappeared into the New Orleans morning.

thirteen hours to texas

j. m. redmann

THE NIGHT WAS DARK, THE piney woods of western Louisiana black shadows just beyond the reach of headlight beams. Before me a steam of taillights changed this night into something surreal, rush hour after midnight in the middle of nowhere. All of us fleeing a storm.

New Orleans was always a haunted city, its old walls having witnessed centuries of the dead and the dying, disease, yellow jack and cholera, slavery and poverty, floods and fire, the ones that have touched the close years, racial violence, AIDS.

It's a city that learned if this is all there is, iko, iko, let's keep dancing, let's play the horn in the whorehouse, bury the dead with jazz. Old Man River just keeps rolling along.

At fourteen I heard the banshee winds of Camille. We stayed then. My parents died before I was able to ask why, was it that they didn't know how bad it could be, because by the time they did it was safer to stay than leave? My father took a picture of me that night, reading by a Coleman lantern, the next day one at the water line, almost at the top of the hill where our house was.

I talked to my sister who talked to someone still there, in Ocean Springs, Mississippi; they said the house is still standing. But even if it is, so much of the rest of my young life is gone, those permanent buildings ephemeral.

What would I really miss? I asked myself, as I packed that day. Category 5 in the Gulf, heading for New Orleans. I hadn't left before, but now it was time. If it's not here tomorrow, what will I most regret losing? Living through Camille, coming out of our house, that next bright day, seeing how close the water had come to us, how the water and the wind destroyed so easily what it had touched, I knew that there was no guarantee that grace would visit me a second time. I packed with a chill seeping into my heart—it might not be here, my little world, my house, my possessions, the city itself.

My computer, a desktop, I could replace; I left it, stored everything on a jump drive. Same with the stereo. I did grab a bunch of CDs, more for the drive than to preserve. Clothes, of course, but not just a grab of summer, late August summer things, but also sweaters and jackets, the ones I liked and would miss if I couldn't wrap myself in them in the next November winds.

Books. A few to read, although I didn't. Life became too real for fiction to enter in those months that followed. Copies of all of mine, heavy boxes that sat in the trunk of my car, safe with me as I traveled, wondering if home might become a bookshelf and some donated furniture.

Two paintings, one of the rabbit, a Walter Anderson woodcut that I bought at fourteen, when I worked at Shearwater Pottery—I liked the colors, how the black blocks had been painted in, the alert yet calm way the rabbit was peering over its shoulder. The other, painted by Walter's younger brother, Mac Anderson, a shrimp boat passing an inlet in the marsh. They were pieces of my past I didn't want to let go.

A few other things, peanut butter and jam, a big knife, an even bigger flashlight, a blanket. Survival. Thinking maybe if I was prepared, fate, seeing that I was not tempting it, would be kind.

I left late, hoping for a last-minute turning, a weakening, and because I could, no pets or weak or older family members, only myself to care for, a car in decent shape.

The first bands of the storm caught me just beyond the city, where I sat stuck in unmoving traffic on the Bonnet Carré Spillway. The rain lashed as I sat immobile on a ribbon of concrete, water of the lake on one side, swamp below and on the other side. Traffic finally moved again, but the rain stayed with me, a dark hovering cloud constantly in my rearview mirror, until the day turned to night and everything became black and rainy.

I learned to drive a different way, put the car in first gear, a little gas, then shift back into neutral and coast, save gas, save my knee. Turn the air conditioning off, sweat it out, don't pee it out, keep the engine from over heating. It was hot that day, mid-90s, hours of sitting in traffic with the beating sun glaring overhead.

Thirteen hours to the Texas border, it's usually five. In the heat and the rain and the traffic, rest areas blocked with too many cars, all desperately trying to stop and rest for a moment. Or perhaps they have no other place to go.

Thirteen hours to Texas, the border between the states. The first exit is the one I take, the kindness of friends. I call them from the gas station, too exhausted to follow the directions they've given me to their house. It is past midnight and the rush-hour traffic continues to speed by. I came to Texas because it was closest— of the places I was offered haven. It was a choice that became meaningless: I thought I would be returning in a few days and I thought that Texas would be the shortest drive.

Instead I sat in Shelley's and Connie's living room watching on TV as my city flooded, streets that were once familiar became brackish bayous, and New Orleans became haunted with more souls. Not just the ghosts of the dead, although they alone are a burden almost beyond bearing, but every house filled with water to the roof, all the talismans of memory, from baby pictures to flags taken from the coffins of veterans, all gone. Gone with the water. Apocalypse now on Bourbon Street. We all know what it means to miss New Orleans.

And the TV cameras couldn't begin to capture all of it, this biblical flood, a diaspora not seen in this country since the Civil War. The cameras, rightly so, focused on the worst of the horrors—sweltering babies and elderly trapped with fear instead of food, worry instead of water, in the City That Care Forgot in a nation that forgot to care. The cameras captured the bloated bodies floating in the stagnant water, desperate people being saved from rooftop hells, aerial views of roofs touching water, sputtering officials with no answers to questions that demanded answers.

Most of us who fled did so out of camera range. We made it to friends and family, a spare bedroom, a sleeper couch, an air mattress, not the desperation of the shelters. Most of us watched, just as the rest of the nation—and even world—did. But we watched not in fascinated horror, we watched for glimpse of our homes, the building where we worked, we watched the grocery store we went to being looted, water where we used to stand and call, "Throw me something, mister," our doctor's office, our bank, our favorite restaurant—every place where we lived out lives, from the mundane of the corner drugstore to the corner where we fell in love. We watched it all turn to a watery hell and we watched our lives change forever. We had food and water and air conditioning and we weren't desperate and no camera caught our anguish as we lost everything except our very lives.

Connie and Shelley were kind and offered to let me stay, but Texas was not my home—I had no home that I could be sure of, so I choose travel—if I was going somewhere maybe it would blunt that I had no place to return from that journey. Friends and family were kind, with offers from Jeane in Arkansas, Susan in North

Carolina (my family had let her stay with us when her family's house had been destroyed by Camille—she e-mailed me to say she owed me lodging), Debbie in Virginia, Pat in Philadelphia, Maude and Rock in New York City, Michaela in Boston, Nancy in Colorado, Lori in Seattle, even offers in Frankfurt, Germany and Barcelona, Spain.

But even travel can be wearying, and this was not travel of my choice, and I ended up staying for most of the time in Arkansas, partly because it was still within a day's drive to New Orleans—even if that wasn't my home any more I still had ties that would need to be dealt with—partly because I was able to work there. My friend had a computer that she was generous with, a spare bedroom and a spare bathroom. Being middle-class means my friends tend to be middle-class, and they have comfortable homes, with extra bedrooms. My personal diaspora wasn't one of physical discomfort, crammed into a shelter, or staying with family in an already too-crowded house.

From afar I watched, gleaning scraps of information. Maybe my house hadn't flooded; the maps seemed to indicate the water stopped close to where I lived. My house was high and it began to seem likely that the water may not have gotten in. But I lived close to Canal Street, the French Quarter, the places that were looted. Even if I escaped the flood, had my roof held in the wind, had the vandals passed me by?

And even if I escaped, had a personal reprieve, New Orleans had not. Too many people had lost too much. Houses, jobs, business, schools, utterly gone, blacked moldy ghosts of buildings. Even being okay in the midst of that much loss is not the same thing as being really okay.

In mid-October, before the water was fit to drink, I drove down to the city, to finally know what had happened to my small piece of it. Again, the kindness of friends: I stopped in Hammond, about forty-five minutes out of the city, and spent the night there. My friend Greg was house sitting and Michael, the owner, had told him it was okay if his friends stayed there. Kindness from strangers. We talked and we laughed and we cried, and drank more than we should, but damn it, we were from New Orleans, and that's how people from New Orleans have always coped.

The day was bright and sunny, it was hard to find gas, the traffic on the North Shore was beyond heavy, it took me an hour to get to the Lake Pontchartrain Causeway. And then the tollbooth operator waved me through; they weren't collecting tolls and it was just me and a few other cars. Six weeks since I had been home, since I had left on the hurried day to drive into the endless night to Texas.

As I neared the shore, I could begin to see the damage, the windblown rips of signs and buildings, and this was the suburb, on the side where the floodwall had held.

It was the middle of the day, a bright blue October. The traffic was light as I merged onto the interstate, more suited to the late hours of night into early morning. Debris still littered the side of the road, signs askew or gone.

When I came into the city itself, passing the battered Superdome—its roof still streaked and torn—in a reverse of the midnight rush hour that had taken me from here, after I passed the exit to the Westbank, no one was on the highway, just me and one other car. This was I-10 in the Downtown heart of New Orleans. Just two cars.

The Indigo Girls song "Ghosts" came on. "There's not enough room in this world for my pain," they sang as I drove into my ruined city.

I barely recognized the exit to Esplanade Avenue, the trees mangled or gone, watermarks on the now visible buildings.

Trash was everywhere, big, reeking piles in the shaded median of Esplanade Avenue. None of the stoplights worked. The gas station where I stopped to fill up had a boat next to the pump where I used to pull my car.

I took a turn and then another turn and was on Barracks Street, past the stop sign to my block. Then in front of my house. Cars in the street had lines showing where the water had been, there were shingles scattered along the sidewalk, branches had been pushed out of the road onto the curb. But then I noticed that the azaleas planted in front of my house were green and alive. The water had not made it up the slanted sidewalk to them.

The air itself spoke of what had changed, heavy with mixed decays, fallen trees, their leaves going back to earth, the reek of rotten meat and mold setting in.

I walked up the stairs, fumbled for the key I hadn't used in close to two months—I'd had to search them out to take with me.

I opened the door. It was still there, my bookcases still filled with books, everything seemingly as I had left it. The roof had held, the water had not come it. New Orleans had not escaped, but I had.

Clearly someone had been inside: I had closed all the doors and they were now open. As I ventured to the back, I discovered that the back door had been pried open. At first I assumed that it had been the police, given the methodical way the doors had been opened, but then I noticed things missing, a jewelry case left open, the heavy brass magnifier by my computer gone.

It probably was the police who had first broken the door, but someone had followed them, grabbing what they could. Jewelry and liquor—they had taken the good Scotch, all my booze in fact, save for the beer in the refrigerator. I was caught between feeling relief that they had only taken cheap and unused jewelry, which could be easily replaced, and being offended that the rest of my stuff had been dismissed as worthless. Mostly it was relief. Mostly I just stood in the silence of the house and marveled that everything I feared lost hadn't been. I had imagined a bed of blooming mold, walls and paintings streaked from a damaged roof, the fury of vandals who destroyed what they didn't take.

The lights were on, the phone even worked. No gas, so no cooking or heat or washing clothes. The refrigerator . . . I tried to clean it, I spent hours gloved and masked, with bleach and insecticide and walking outside every once in a while to breathe air that wasn't so rancid. After hours, and my back was hurting and I could only wash my hands with bottled water and that hand sanitizer stuff, I gave up and called my landlord. I didn't even get a chance to tell him that I didn't think the refrigerator couldn't be saved before he told me he was getting a new one. The kindness of landlords.

I stayed the night, couldn't drink the water, although late in the day the officials announced that you could. I did risk a shower in it, warm enough still that not having any hot water was only noticeable instead of blue-butt freezing-cold miserable. Somewhere in my tool kit, I found a security chain for a door; I put in on the back one, its lock destroyed. I also found a stout board that I shoved under the doorknob, then weighed that down with my exercise bike. The night was too dark to risk letting it come in.

Couldn't cook, couldn't keep food cold. I ate packed cheese and crackers and trail mix for dinner and again for breakfast the following morning, washed down with tepid Diet Pepsi for the necessary caffeine.

When I left that morning my first thought was just to drive away, but I swerved at the last moment, instead taking the extra minutes to drive by places I had known. Where I worked. One small office near the French Quarter looked okay; it hadn't been flooded. But the main office, I'd already seen it surrounded by the flood in pictures. It was desolate when I drove by. I was the only car along that long stretch of Tulane Avenue. The building was striped with dirty water lines, the darkest where the water was highest, then lower ones as it was slowly pumped out. Windows were broken, like a face beaten and bruised. Nothing was green— all the grass and trees had sat for too long in the brackish water. Overturned cars had been piled by the edge of the road.

Near the French Quarter, where I live, people had been out working, cleaning, clearing. The stoplight at Esplanade and North

Rampart had been fixed since the night before. But here, there was nothing, no one was working to resurrect this lonely stretch. I took a few pictures, not so much for me—I wouldn't forget this—but to show others what I had seen, to have a chance to explain how these destroyed places seared me.

Then I got back on the interstate and drove back to Hammond to spend a civilized night with Greg as we again drank and laughed, and somehow decided that we and New Orleans had a future.

I drove up to Arkansas the next day, almost got there, but then blew a tire outside of Hernando, Mississippi, and had to spend three hours there at the Wal-Mart—there wasn't much else there—while they fixed it. While I was waiting at the gas station for the tow truck, a man came up to me. "Katrina?" he asked, seeing my license plate. He was from Bay St. Louis. I told him my story, he told me his. Strangers at a gas station, he needed someone who knew.

It was one of the things I noticed in the months that followed, how much we all needed to tell our stories, as if we all knew how important this was, how each story added up to something so much bigger than just stories. Trapped on a roof, rescued and finally getting clean underwear after a week; finding a grandmother's body in the wreckage of a home; blowing up condoms, putting them in a garbage bag to get through the water; how did you do, where did you go? We all told our stories.

I'm back in New Orleans now, the long lines, the long drives, past block after block after block of ghost homes. Three grocery stores are open in the city. For the first two months I was here, I had to drive halfway across town to pick up my mail—I've had to create a form letter to send out about late fees. Like most here, I'm lucky if I get the bill a few days before it's due. Now mail is delivered a few days a week, only first class, no magazines. That was my break from work to home, sitting on the futon and reading a few articles. Sometimes I can find a *National Geographic* at the grocery store and I try to make do with that.

But the loss that I drive by every day makes it impossible to complain, makes me realize that, while some things will be hard for me, I'll be okay. Others won't be. For some, it may be a long, hard road. Others have lost too much and nothing in this lifetime will ever bring it back. In New Orleans, always a haunted city, now even the newer parts have too many ghosts.

Six months and the water lines are still here. Too many of the people are gone. The rest of us hold on to some fragile high ground, not just of the earth but of our souls.

And hurricane season will come again this June and the levees will be only as high as they were before and it's still thirteen hours to Texas.

joy: wind, water, worms

kay murphy

I. 25–26 SEPTEMBER 1998

Two raggedy blue corrugated tin sheds,
broken rusted hinged doors, flank our back yard
shaking, rattling, yes, even rolling up
thundering like the sound track for *The Tempest*
when Hurricane Georges begins to grow fat on

fronts and fear. You roll the TV from the closet
listen to a twenty-four-hour weather channel,
terrorize yourself with ads for ill women
over forty while Georges' numbers rising
falling rising send you seasick to our bed.

That night we stick it out with windows, doors, ply-
boarded while motels west of New Orleans
triple room rates; batteries disappear from
Ace's hardware; the only candles we can
find are printed with *O La Milagrosa*

Madre mia hear my perpetual sin-
cere petition: *Please do not make me spend my*
birthday in exile. All that day we argue
over whether we should stay or leave. *Stay*, I
plead, Midwesterner without much water sense.

Desperate to please me, you ask one neighbor,
Elsie, in her eighties, stooped, and her daughter
bald now, breast mutilated, swinging on the porch
with a smoke, if they intend to stay. Elsie,
asks her daughter, who says, *When Betsy hit*

the skating rink collapsed and ruined my life.
Having once outsmarted death in the sixties,
they are not budging. The gay guys across the street
are staying now the storm has dropped to a two.
You are beginning to give. *Disaster makes*

community. One breath later, you are all
panic; your eyes bulge; you have palpitations.
I give up my Odyssean pride to face
the one-eyed monster. Better to ride bumper
to bumper than be boarded up inside with

a lover bent on blaming me for five deaths.
(Three of them cats). If I'm wrong (which I'm not)
we'll all die; you'll have no pleasure in being right,
as I would. So up we pack (or I should say

I do, since you have secreted a room in

Tuscaloosa and stowed your overnight case,
packed, under the bed. How many couples break
up during a hurricane? Two cat carriers,
one stone silent grudge holder slouched passenger
side, who makes you drive the two hundred twenty-

five miles northeast starting at midnight while Georges
shadows us and the fire ants who have taken
asylum in the car crawl inside my socks.

II. 30 SEPTEMBER 1998

Returning three days later, (having partied
for my birthday in a Shoney's Inn with a
Little Debbie punctured with a white candle),
I drive. Mattresses and carpets already
piled in soggy heaps along the roadside

east, the low side of New Orleans, where it
is as quiet as the inside of an eye.
Even the skinny dogs seem murky looking.
Our house, dark in daylight, seventy-six hours
without electricity, the garbage brought

in to keep from battering the neighbor's Ram,
wriggles with maggots. Because I don't believe
in killing anything, I get the task of
wheeling them to the kitchen door, slowly, so
none will be shaken from the can's slick sides,

carrying the can down four steps without them
touching me, sticking to my clothes; rolling

the can down the broken concrete driveway,
detouring around the car; walking back on
the other side in case some had fallen off.

You have bathed, gone to bed, your cat rising,
falling with your breasts. The refrigerator
waits, stinks of slimy greens turned brown, a green
oval that once shone yellow—what the sun did
last time I saw it. I guess I deserve this,

although nothing I eat spoils. I amass
the placenta-looking mess in plastic, leave
it for the maggots who by morning will be
buzzing *Feed me too* at the steamy window,
and I'll wonder when our killer storm will hit.

I don't bathe, but sit in my study surrounded
by wet fur smell of words. Just last week you said,
Let's make a plan next time, but I don't believe
in them. This season some of us were spared.
The Times-Picayune says it's because of prayers,

Voodoo, and *el Niño*. What could have swamped this
city turned away. Things are still good, but
the Gulf Coast holds its breath 'til further notice.

for Joyce

•

"WIND, WATER, WORMS" IS FROM a series called *The
Ascent of Joy* taken from a line by Delmore Schwartz, "Writing is
the ascent of joy." The poems were inspired by a pair of numbers,

five and eleven. I'm working with five-line stanzas with lines that average eleven syllables. Several of the poems are eleven stanzas long. This poem is eighty-six lines, which, in numerology equals five. Of the eleven-poem series, about half of them—all in earlier drafts—were rescued by a friend who managed to get an illegal "business" pass, go into my apartment in Mid-City, and grab a handful of disks from my desk.

As I worked through the poem, remembering some of the revisions I had made, I was struck by the attitude of the speaker, an aspect of myself who feigns a nonchalant persona in times of impending doom. At the time of its genesis, during Hurricane Georges, I felt pretty much like the speaker of the poem: The worst disaster I would encounter would be to cancel theater plans for my birthday. Yet I also understood a hurricane disaster was inevitable.

I did not intuit that truth again until the Saturday morning of August 27, 2005, when Brad Richard called to say he would not be at our poetry workshop that afternoon because he and his partner were evacuating. I said, "What for?" Like many others, I was not aware that Katrina had turned her force in our direction during the night. Brad said nothing to frighten me; I simply knew the time had come. The breath we had all been holding for seven years, or perhaps holding since Hurricane Betsy, was about to exhale in such force that the now-famous refrigerators—only a receptacle for spoiled food in Georges—would be swimming on their backs in kitchens all along the Gulf Coat. I packed my cat, a half-dozen books (out of more than 3,000), a photo of my son and me, one of the Dalai Lama, and clothes for four days.

KAY MURPHY
19 MARCH 2006
FITHIAN, ILLINOIS (POPULATION 550)

a home away from home

toni amato and amie m. evans

AS WRITERS AND ACTIVISTS, WE know all too well how difficult it can be to find places and spaces that feel like home. Places where all the ways our queer voices speak can be heard, places in which all the various aspects of our queer sensibilities are welcomed and honored. Places where we can be whole and where the things we hold most sacred are cherished are holy places. Paul Willis has made a home for us, and he has made it in New Orleans.

TONI

THIS YEAR, 2006, WILL BE my third time attending Saints and Sinners. In a literary time and place where so few LGBTQ conferences exist, or are truly as inclusive as they claim to be, I look forward to Saints and Sinners as my true literary home.

My first year was 2004. I had just edited *Pinned Down by Pronouns*, and fought through the firestorm of scandal that rocked the Lambda Literary Awards. After a full year spent collecting and honing the voices of over seventy-five LGBTQ writers who claimed space in the gender variant world, I was heartbroken by the tragedy that was Michael Bailey's hateful book. Once again, the voices I loved most deeply seemed destined to remain homeless while yet another outsider presumed to speak for them—until Paul Willis began the Saints and Sinners Literary Festival in New Orleans.

I sat in sweltering heat, in an outdoor courtyard, and finally heard fellow writers stand up for transgender and intersex issues. I listened as panelists and workshop leaders, along with conference attendees, included all the letters in our ever increasingly queer alphabet soup. Even as a dyed-in-the-wool New Englander who prefers snowdrifts to flying cockroaches and peanut brittle to pralines, I spent those all too brief two days feeling more like I had come home than gone visiting.

New Orleans has always beckoned those of us who are from away as the place where all of our freakishness is acceptable, where pride and love and a spirit of celebration are what matters most.

One night, Amie and I walked past the back of Saint Louis Cathedral, the enormous shadow of a well-lit statue of Christ looming over the wall. I stopped in my tracks, aware of His presence like never before. His upraised hands welcomed me back home. I had no time to enter the cathedral that year, but in 2005 I walked the Stations of the Cross, admiring the stained glass images of His suffering, and wondering yet again how I could ever really know what He had done for me. As I walked, I knew that this place would be holy ground for me, where the things most dear to me would be held sacred. New Orleans would forever feel like home.

And yet, tourist I was. Flocks of sparrows swam through the thick hot air. Buskers with tattoos and serpents seemed far more exotic than my own Harvard Square street musicians. I packed on a good five pounds in deep-fried pickles and pralines. Most of my time was spent in the French Quarter and, yes, I did buy a set of Mardi Gras beads.

The cameras were rolling after Katrina struck. So many pictures of so much suffering and loss. Homelessness of a far different kind made as real as film and cyberspace could make it. And although I sat vigil for the survivors and Mass for the dead, I still was a tourist. I can never allow myself to forget that what I did as the storm blew through and the aftermath began was to watch. I watched a National Guardsmen climb the statue of the Christ whose fingers had been broken off in the storm, yet who still held His arms open. I watched.

I watched as residents took up for each other, took care of each other, and even found reasons to celebrate. I watched as New Orleans citizens fought to keep their homes. I watched a bravery I cannot begin to fathom and a compassion that took me back to that night in back of the cathedral. What I know of the damage and suffering is still only what I know from a flat screen atop my desk. I know enough to know that I will be visiting a New Orleans forever changed. I know enough to know that all I can do is witness, but as E.L. Doctorow said, "We need writers to witness to this terrifying century."

AMIE

HUMID AND SUNNY NEW ORLEANS is full of tropical plants I love but cannot grow in my New England garden: elephant ears, palm and banana trees, lush green vegetation and blooming flowers in pinks, whites, reds, and yellows all year long. The shotgun, single-story homes have ceiling-to-floor doors instead of windows on the front porches to allow as much of a breeze in as possible and have shutters to cover them in case of bad weather. And the old estates with their center courtyards once used for receiving guests in horse-drawn carriages are now converted into open-air coffee houses. So unlike the buttoned-down, buttoned-up Puritan Boston I love with its storm windows and snow, its cabbages growing in the municipal gardens in the fall, its clam chowder and Fenway park hotdogs.

Food is like a religion in New Orleans, served up in lavish dishes full of rich flavors and texture, with pride and love. My beloved chowder is winter pale compared to sassy Creole cooking. Dishes like jambalaya and étouffée delight in mixing regional delicacies with items brought from distant assorted places. Everyone who comes to New Orleans is welcomed and mixed into the gumbo pot. So it was true of me. New Orleans—hot tropical, lush, green—felt welcoming, comfortable, and accepting.

On my first walking tour of the cemeteries, the last stop was a botanica with a voodoo temple. Nature, Christianity, and ancient religions form the old continent mixed together over the centuries into voodoo. I filed into the courtyard with twenty other tourists, drank the cold water offered, listened to the priestess speak her words of wisdom and, when the other tourists started asking questions, I broke away to go into the altar room. I placed on the altar a piece of candy, a dollar bill, and a cigarette, the customary offerings for the Loas.

I do not believe in these gods any more than I believe in the Christian God of my childhood. What I do believe in is the faith that the followers of any god have in their deities. It is that faith I honor just as I honored the Christian God in the Saint Louis Cathedral.

On our last afternoon in New Orleans, Toni and I watched an awe-inspiring thunderstorm move in from the second-floor balcony of a restaurant on Bourbon Street. The dark, ominous clouds rolled in over the Downtown skyscrapers. So slow was their approach that we finished eating our shrimp po'boys before picking up our drinks and stepping into the restaurant as the edge of the clouds engulfed the sky above us, turning the area to twilight. We watched from the open veranda doors as the rain fell in sheets onto the tables, buildings, and street, and lightning flashed bright before everything fell again into a soupy brown. And then, as quickly as it had come, the storm left. The air was fresh and clean and the sky was clear and sunny. We joked, two New Englanders used to Nor'easters, about how kind Mother Nature was to New Orleans, blessing her with sun and cleansing flash rains.

The week Katrina hit the Gulf Coast, I was in New Hampshire at a time-share with my partner and friends, tucked away in a golf resort safe from the bustle of the world—or so I thought. I hadn't even brought my phone book. I was planning to spend the first part of the week socializing and relaxing and the second half alone writing. The cable TV showed pictures of Katrina hitting New Orleans. The French Quarter was immediately recognizable to those of us who had been there. The images of the wind and the rain and folks attempting to get out of the city made us sad and worried. Worried about the historical houses we had toured. Worried about the cemeteries and vulnerable centuries-old tombs. Worried about friends and acquaintances— had they gotten out safely?

The stories that trickled in on NPR during the weeks after Katrina truly tore my heart apart. Stories from the displaced survivors about what they had lost or left behind and hoped to recover.

Two survivors' tales have stuck with me even now. The first is that of a man in his mid-thirties, a photographer who had lost all of his equipment and had been airlifted to Cape Cod. Local folks donated equipment to allow him to continue with his art. But, he had lost all his work, all his negatives. New pictures he could take, but the creativity he had put into the original work was gone.

The second was the story of a sixtysomething, African-American man who had written poetry about his family, their experiences, the high and low points in their live, and his remembrances and feelings on the world his whole life. He'd written all of it longhand on paper with no computer back-up. All of it was destroyed. None of it can be passed on to his children to give to their children's children. A lifetime of artistic energy of love and life captured washed away, turned into pulpy mush, just gone.

•

AND THEN THERE IS PAUL Willis. Paul is, for us, the embodiment of the collective spirit that will save New Orleans after Katrina. In 2004, Paul worked without pay to create the Saints and Sinners Literary Festival, a fundraiser for NO/AIDS. Only a few days afterwards, in the very home he had opened to all of us, in the heart of the French Quarter itself, he was attacked and beaten. Several young men with bats jumped from a van and beat Paul Willis so severely that he lost the sight in one of his eyes. If not for three teenage girls who ran out of a café and yelled, causing the assailants to run off, he might have been killed. Paul nevertheless worked to make Saints and Sinners 2005 a reality. More than 150 LGBTQ writers once more met for three days of master classes, panel discussions, readings, and a celebration of LGBTQ literature.

But Paul and his home were not to know peace. Hurricane Katrina struck, forcing Paul, his partner, and their cat to leave their home and belongings for months. Not knowing where some of their friends were or if they were safe. Not knowing if their home or belongings would be there when they returned. And yet always sure they would return. And return he did.

Now, Paul works to make S&S continue in 2006, to bring LGBTQ writers back to New Orleans, even as he prepares to have his eye removed and works to fix the damage to his home. Paul won't let anything stop him. Paul Willis's spirit is that which will conquer the AIDS pandemic, will overcome the silencing effects of homophobia, and will celebrate the joy of community. That same spirit will ensure that New Orleans is returned to its pre-Katrina grandeur. Perhaps, stronger and wiser from her experiences, less racially- and class-divided. She will not allow herself to be dispirited or stopped. Like Paul, she will get up and continue to thrive. What other option could there possibly be?

the fear of tides

martin pousson

When we return to the Café du Monde,
we'll find no one speaks English anymore—

a language too heavy
for a sinking city. When we return

to eat *beignets* after dark, speaking
Old French, the table will be overcast

with clouds of powdered sugar. Beads of mist will spray
from the river, sparkle in the lampglow

of the café, and the air will fill
with the humming confession that we are

too much like the city we live in.
Unimpressed by the roar of mosquitoes,

the buzz of hurricanes, we'll sit
in wrought-iron chairs at the Café du Monde

and no one will leave, not even when we hear
the Mississippi is swelling. No one

in New Orleans wonders aloud if the city
will sink, no one mentions the fear

of tides. Polite as anyone,
neither will we—baptized in a faith

taboo to question. And when the river,
the artery of New Orleans bursts,

we'll sink with the city before we admit
our return to the Café du Monde is the end.

all on a mardi gras day

dr. jon lohman

THIS TUESDAY, FEBRUARY 28, [2006] will mark the six-month anniversary of Katrina's initial destructive arrival in New Orleans. In true New Orleans Carnival-esque fashion, this anniversary falls not on just any Tuesday, but rather on the day before Ash Wednesday, Shrove Tuesday, better known as "Fat Tuesday," "Carnival," or Mardi Gras. The New Orleans Mardi Gras is one of America's largest tourist attractions and greatest public spectacles, attracting visitors from all over the globe, who make the pilgrimage to experience Carnival's notoriously lascivious and permissive atmosphere. New Orleans's Carnival is celebrated concurrently in cities throughout Europe in cities such as Venice, Munich, and Nice, and famously in the Caribbean and South American cities of Port of Spain, Port-au-Prince, and Rio de Janeiro. With the recent catastrophic events of Katrina and her aftermath, however, there has been much heated public debate as to whether New Orleans should have a Mardi Gras this year.

On the surface, various calls to cancel Mardi Gras appear well justified. A full six months after the storm, the Crescent City still finds itself in many respects on its knees—about half of the city is still without power, entire neighborhoods remain abandoned, many curbsides are still piled high with the contents of gutted-out homes, streets are still littered with thousands of abandoned flooded-out cars, few schools and hospitals have reopened, many streetlights are still out, and tens of thousands of residents are left waiting in a maddening sea of red tape for insurance adjustments and the necessary permits required to begin to rebuild their lives.

The very question of whether or not to *have* Mardi Gras, however, is flawed from the outset. A better question might be whether or not the city will choose to *observe* Mardi Gras, for Mardi Gras, one of America's oldest holidays, will take place regardless of how we choose to honor it. Its annual date is not chosen by city government, law enforcement, or the tourism and hospitality industry, but is rather subject to the annual fluctuations of the Christian calendar. Specifically, Mardi Gras falls forty-seven days before Easter, on the day before Ash Wednesday. Carnival, whose name is derived from the Latin roots *carne vale*, "farewell to flesh," has for centuries marked the final day of excess and indulgence before the Lenten period. And while Carnival's connection to the religious observance of Lent has admittedly greatly diminished over the years, it has remained an a kind of cultural "steam valve," a welcomed cathartic release and a liberating "time out of time."

Mardi Gras creates a festive space of playful paradoxes, where children can act like adults, and adults can act like children. It marks a time when debutantes can dress in burlesque, when the most conservative businessman can go in drag, when whites can masquerade in blackface, and black can wear whiteface, or even assume the identity of a "Wild Indian." It permits a collective license for "masking," while affording the possibility of numerous "unmaskings" as well, as many participants shed their "everyday" public personas and wear their usually hidden private desires on their sleeves. The Russian literary critic Mikhail Bakhtin beautifully described Carnival in his seminal classic *Rabelais and His World* as a festive ritual governed by "the peculiar logic of the 'inside out' of the 'turnabout,' of a continual shifting from top to bottom, from front to rear, of numerous parodies and travesties, humiliations, profanations, comic crownings and uncrownings." During Mardi Gras, a spirit of license is not only perceived by its participants, but is accompanied by a tangible relaxation of many "everyday" regulations of public behavior. During Carnival, many activities that are normally frowned upon are not just tolerated but arguably celebrated. "Regular" business hours are disrupted, schools are closed, and the city experiences a near tripling in population.

Carnival is attended by both young and old, locals and tourists, men and women, blacks and whites—and so often blurs, twists, inverts, confuses, and otherwise challenges these dichotomous distinctions. Mardi Gras becomes virtually all-encompassing, and even those residents who typically dread the wild crowds of Carnival season find that they must temporarily yield to Carnival's control over much of this city's public spaces. "While Carnival lasts," Bakhtin observed, "there is no other life outside it. It has a universal spirit; it is a special condition of the entire world, of the world's revival and renewal, in which all take part."

I got my first taste of the pivotal place that Mardi Gras holds in the lives of many New Orleanians when I moved there to teach in a public school as a member of Teach for America. A few other first-year teachers and I rented an apartment in a house Uptown, a half-block off Napoleon Avenue. Our landlord, a Baton Rouge attorney who had grown up in the home, walked us through the rental agreement, spending an unusually long time on a particular clause at the expense of others. During Mardi Gras, the clause read, our landlord and any of his friends had the non-negotiable right to enter our home, unannounced, and use the toilet in our basement. He was an officer of the Krewe of Endymion, (third float, neutral ground side) he explained, as was his father and his father before him, and one can never know when one might need a bathroom during Mardi Gras. While he never took advantage of this unique breaking-and-entering clause in the years we spent in that apartment, he always made it the central focus of our lease extensions.

I soon learned that my landlord was not unique in the way his participation in Carnival steered much of his personal identity. Mardi Gras, for many, is more or less a year-round enterprise, whether one is a member of one of the many competitive school marching bands, or decorating one of their homemade floats for the annual "truck parades," or going through the tryouts to become a "flambeau," the torch-bearing men who still carry on the tradition of African-Americans who illuminated the first torch-lit parades nearly 150 years ago.

Along with the wide range of possibilities for participation in city-sanctioned parades, many of the most vibrant and resilient expressive Carnival traditions have developed and thrived outside of official Mardi Gras activities. The harsh racial restrictions of Jim Crow limited blacks' participation in Mardi Gras to the carrying of the flambeau. The result was a transgressive, largely secretive development of African-American festive traditions, including the rise of African-American benevolent societies, or "social aid and pleasure clubs." These groups continue to serve as critical social organizations in their neighborhoods, and the primary sponsors of "second lines," the highly participatory street parades that follow the pulsating brass-band beats through New Orleans's back streets. Out of Jim Crow also arose the remarkable tradition of the Mardi Gras Indians, African-Americans who spend the better part of the year constructing intricately sewn "Indian suits" of beads, feathers, and sequins. Organized into "Uptown" and "Downtown" tribes led by their "Big Chief," the Indians don their new suits on Mardi Gras morning and set out with their "spyboys," "flagboys," and "wildmen" to engage in highly ritualized confrontations with other tribes to determine who is the "prettiest." Though having gained a significant amount of notoriety for their artistry (the late Big Chief Allison "Tootie" Montana was honored with the National Heritage Fellowship in 1987) the Indians have consistently resisted the city's attempts to incorporate them into mainstream Mardi Gras.

As city officials debated the structure and schedule of official Mardi Gras festivities, their conclusions have had little or no bearing on when, where, and how the Mardi Gras Indian tribes choose to hit the streets on Mardi Gras morning. The same could also be said for the dizzying number of other "unofficial" Mardi Gras organizations, such as the blissfully irreverent Society of Saint Anne, the Krewe of Cosmic Debris, the Jefferson City Buzzards, Pete Fountain's Half-Fast Walking Club, or the Krewe of Julu, a raucous band of klezmer music–led revelers, who follow the Zulu Parade and their much coveted golden coconuts with their own offering of gold-painted bagels. "In New Orleans," local photographer and cultural scholar Michael P. Smith has keenly observed, "culture is not cast down from on high, but bubbles up from the street." And the word on the street is that most of these deeply cherished neighborhood traditions are going to proceed, even if the neighborhoods themselves remain in ruins.

To those taking in the Mardi Gras festivities from afar, mediated through truncated video clips on their evening news, the sight of these revelers parading through devastated neighborhoods might seem jarring at best, and callous at worst. Witnesses should remember, however, that this is the city that routinely turns its funeral processions into rousing Second Line parades, and often seems to find it preferable to satirize life's calamities and dance in the face of the devil. For probably more than any other American city, New Orleans has cultivated a highly developed "festive vocabulary," and early reports from this year's Carnival indicate that Katrina has done little to temper their satiric wit. The annual

Krewe Du Vieux Parade, much celebrated for its irreverent yet effective political satire, did not disappoint. This year's theme was "C'est Levee," and featured floats that included a comic caricature of a Frenchman at home in New Orleans, with the plea "Buy Us Back Chirac!" Costumes on the street followed suit, with plenty of drag queens dressed in Brownie girl scout uniforms (as in "Heckuva job, Brownie!"), bumbling FEMA agents, and various representations of Mayor Nagin's now infamous vision of a "chocolate city."

Many will continue to argue that, in the wake of Katrina, the city has no business investing their scarce, limited resources in hosting Mardi Gras. Yet, choosing between basic human services and a deeply cherished age-old public celebration is simply not a choice that a modern American city should have to make. The children of New Orleans have seen their schools flooded, their homes ruined, and their neighborhoods irrevocably shattered. Must we take away their Mardi Gras parades as well? New York chose not to cancel the World Series or forgo the annual lighting of the Rockefeller Center Christmas Tree following the tragic events of September 11, largely because they understood that these kinds of public rituals—these festive "times out of time" that connect us with deeply cherished memories and provide a momentary respite from the troubles of the day—take on even greater importance in the wake of public tragedy. And the city officials of New York understood as well the importance of these events to the local economic recovery. The same is desperately true in New Orleans. Well before Katrina, local gift shops, restaurants, hotels, music clubs, and other businesses have relied on a busy Mardi Gras season to pull them through the dog days of summer.

In the peculiar yet beautiful logic that governs the Big Easy, it could very well prove that the observance of Carnival, the grand public homage to disorder, might just signal that things are finally starting to get back to normal in New Orleans. Ultimately, though, the decision of whether or not to celebrate Mardi Gras in New Orleans rests not in the mayor's office or the city council, but rather in the hands of captains, queens, grand marshals, and big chiefs. And they have made their decision clear. Through hell or high water, they're going to roll.

I've got my ticket in my hand. Won't you meet me there?

fur chaps and the candyman

paul j. willis

I HADN'T HAD THE TIME or energy to put much thought into my Mardi Gras costume. I knew several New Orleanians would've though, and I couldn't wait to see their "Katrina creations." My partner was grumbling at me to get moving, so I threw on my ole' reliable—a pair of black and white fur chaps with red fringe down the side that a friend had made. I grabbed my black cowboy hat from Silver Dollar City, and we made our way out the door.

Living in the Lower Garden District, there was no way to get to the French Quarter except to walk up the parade route. The sun was shining, beads were flying, and crowds of locals and tourists were celebrating—celebrating a resilient spirit that is New Orleans. It took us a couple of hours, but we made our way through the crowds and eventually crossed Canal Street and entered the Quarter.

The old streets of the Quarter weren't busting at the seams as in years past. There were still plenty of tourists, but this was a Mardi Gras for the locals. The energy in the air was a bit calmer, more thoughtful. It was as if everyone living in New Orleans collectively took a deep breath and let out all the tension that had been building over the last several months.

My partner and I were headed to Café Lafitte in Exile to meet up with some friends and to take in the scene that is "Fat Tuesday." As we continued our walk up Bourbon Street, I looked over and saw a big smile across his face. I knew what he was thinking. This was the first time since the storm, the evacuation, and the months of uncertainty that it felt like home. This was the New Orleans that enticed us both to move here.

On each block of our trek, we'd run into someone we knew. They too were all smiles. There was no discussion of blue roofs, insurance adjusters, or levee breaches. Instead, the talk was of costume creativity or the admiration of a nice set of pecs that just sauntered by. The inane and silly conversations were a welcome substitute for the dramatic ramblings we'd all been forced to share.

We got to Lafitte's around high noon. The music was blaring and the bar was full. The bulk of the revelers had spilled out on the street, enjoying their drinks and the beautiful weather. We spotted our friends at their usual post. We got a round of drinks and joined in the festivities.

It was a day for men to be boys—playful, mischievous, and flirtatious. After several hours in the sun and a few rounds of drinks, I went into the bar to take a load off. I was fortunate to get a space on the "meat rack" and took a seat. The fur chaps were great for a conversation starter or a nice rub of the hand as folks passed by. They caught the eye of a masked man who made his way over to where I was sitting. He introduced himself and took to rubbing my fur—both the chaps and the hair on my chest.

I welcomed the attention from my new acquaintance. His advances were gentle, yet erotically charged by the mystery of the disguise. His mask was made of leather with a couple of horns on the top. He had a ring through his nose and was wearing a leather harness. I temporarily forgot his name and thought of him as Taurus the bull. The name fit the look and his aggressive style. I called him Taurus as he leaned in and gave me a kiss. He laughed and told me that was the name given to the mask at the leather store where he bought it. He had picked it out because he was a Taurus—his birthday was April 28.

Our connection deepened as I told him my birthday was also April 28. The erotic tension was temporarily broken as we were both taken aback by the coincidence. The conversation opened up freely as if we'd known each other much longer than the ten minutes we'd just spent together. I discovered he owned his own candy store in rural Indiana and that he was in town for Mardi Gras with his partner. They had come to celebrate and show support for the city.

He genuinely wanted to know, so I shared my evacuation experience. I relayed that my partner and I had fled the city the day before the storm hit. How our decision was expedited as soon as they came on the television stating "that if you're going to stay, you need to have an axe so that you can chop yourself out of the roof when the floods come." I shared how the first thirty miles took eight hours in traffic, that people were escaping in various modes of transportation—limos, taxis, moving trucks. I even saw a seven-year-old boy driving a truck while his dad was hooking up the directional lights on their trailer.

The conversation evolved to where we talked about our respective partners, our relationship philosophies, and our growing attraction for each other. And just as the energy had shifted back to a sense of desire, his partner walked up and introduced himself. He was a nice guy and I enjoyed meeting him, but I was more into exploring the connection that had been developing with *the bull*. I wasn't too disappointed though because I knew we had just been sharing a random "New Orleans" moment. The three of us talked for a bit more until the boyfriend mentioned that they needed to go meet a friend for a bite to eat.

I walked out with them when we ran into my partner. I introduced them to each other and thought that would be the last I'd see of the candy maker from Indiana. As his partner headed out into the crowd, he lagged behind to tell me something. He leaned in and told me that his name was the same as my partner's, and that he'd be back in a couple of hours to find me—the same birthday, the coincidence of the last name. I knew that he meant it.

The afternoon progressed with more rounds of drinks, costume critiques, and the mood that things were *easy* again. Our group decided for a change of venue and headed up the street to the Bourbon Parade to listen to some music and dance. Well, my partner wanted to dance. I was a bit buzzed and relaxed. I felt like hanging back to the side of the dance floor to just take in the surroundings and enjoy the mood.

Soon enough, my fur chaps were getting rubbed again. Without turning around to see, I knew that he had found me. I felt the hand move from the fur of the chaps to up and in the backside of my underwear. He rubbed my ass as he leaned in and lightly bit on my ear. He continued down my neck before he turned me around and kissed me hard on the mouth. His eyes were powerful through the leather of the mask, the slight taste of whiskey on his breath. Everything in the background dropped away.

We stayed connected for quite some time, oblivious to our surroundings—kissing deep, rubbing skin, pinching on nipples. For me, all the stress and tension that had been brewing over the last six months just dropped away. It was the first time since the landscape had been altered that I had felt any type of passion. I hadn't thought about sex or physical attraction, but was consumed with raising money for my job or with repairs to the roof of our apartment. I hadn't thought about making new friends, I had been trying to track down old ones scattered across the country.

When we took a break from our exploratory embrace, we both were smiling, almost laughing from the intensity of our connection over the last half hour. We knew that nothing more was going to come of it at this time. He needed to head back up the street to meet up with his boyfriend, and I was with my partner and friends enjoying the day. We decided to move out to the balcony away from the dance floor so that we could talk where it was quieter before he needed to leave.

We found a fairly secluded area towards the end of the balcony. He pulled me towards him again, this time the kiss was much more gentle. He then said it was about time that I saw who I've been spending all this time with. I almost didn't want to break the spell of the mask, but when he pulled it off I saw a very handsome man with kind eyes. He was probably about fifteen years older than I was, with attractive lines around his eyes from having a good disposition. We talked a while longer, and then spent our last ten minutes together just holding hands and watching the street traffic below. He felt comfortable and safe.

My mind drifted from how glad I was to have met this man to all the events that had transpired throughout the day. I was glad to be wearing my fur chaps. I was glad to be home again. In parting, Taurus told me that he'd be back next year for Mardi Gras.

In New Orleans, I bet he'll find me.

i haven't stopped dancing yet

greg herren

I HAVE WRITTEN FIVE NOVELS set in New Orleans, and am currently writing the sixth. In each one, I have taken great pains to make the city as much a character as any of the people— because this strange and exotic city *is* a character. There's no way to write fiction set in New Orleans *without* writing about the city; otherwise, why bother setting it here? Nothing makes me angrier than reading a book set in New Orleans when it is patently obvious the writer never spent more than a weekend here. It is not a generic city, with strip malls and parking lots everywhere you look, with that strangely American sense of sameness so many urban areas seem so bizarrely eager to replicate. When you drive down any street in this city, you *know* you are somewhere different. Yes, we have McDonald's and Wal-Mart and Starbucks, but our chains somehow don't seem as tacky and as obtrusive as they do elsewhere; we take great care to ensure that.

There's this strange magic about New Orleans—our massive swamp oaks and the crumbling narrow streets that somehow seem to transform even the most plastic aspects of generalized American culture into something new and different. Those of us who live here take fierce pride in the city—even as we laugh and shake our heads over its stupidities and insanities and the day to day frustrations that force us to not take life quite as seriously and to slow down . . . what's the point in rushing? You're going to have to wait at some point; here we've even come up with a phrase to describe it: we call it *passin' time*. So why worry? Why get crazed over things? There's no point in hurrying. Kick back and take it easy. What's your rush? It'll be there later, and the world won't come to an end because you didn't get to it five minutes sooner.

Here, we work to live, not live to work.

My love affair with New Orleans began well before I moved here. It was, simply stated, the first place I ever felt at home. Everywhere else I've lived—and there have been plenty of places—I never felt rooted. I never felt loyal. It was just a place to live until I moved on to the next place as I tried to find a place where I fit. I just *belonged* here. Occasionally, when asked why I love the city so much, I smile and say, "I'm not the crazy one here."

I heard the siren song of the crescent city in my heart and made it my physical home as well as my spiritual. I have never once regretted that decision. Nothing makes me happier than when a reviewer remarks on how my "love for New Orleans shines through on every page"—because more than anything else, I want my work to be a homage to this wonderful place. I love New Orleans with all my heart, and I always will.

I've heard it said that life is a dance. For years, I was the wallflower at the prom called life. I stayed home, read books, watched television, and dreamed of the life I wanted so badly I could taste it . . . yet I would never dance. I was a misfit, uncomfortable in my skin, wanting so desperately to belong but never quite getting there. Somehow, no matter where I lived or worked, I didn't quite fit in, so I hid in the shadows, trying not to attract attention, my head down.

It was New Orleans that finally dragged me out onto the dance floor. She beckoned to me, crooking her finger and winking, and I followed her out under the disco ball and laser lights, and began to move my feet to her rhythm.

And I haven't stopped dancing yet.

•

From *www.scottynola.livejournal.com*:
Gone with the Wind [Aug. 28, 2005, 8:58 A.M.]
Hey everyone.
We are packing and getting out of here.
The plan is to go north; we might go as far as Paul's mother's in Illinois.
I don't know when I'll be back online.
Pray for my city, and the people who are unable to leave. There are tens of thousands who have to stay.
God bless you all.

•

I REMEMBER THE EXACT DATE I fell in love with New Orleans. It was my thirty-third birthday: August 20, 1994. I'd been before, but I didn't truly experience the city until that date. On those previous trips, I never *felt* the city; I didn't hear its heartbeat. I'd always found the city fascinating; I loved reading about it in books like *The Witching Hour* by Anne Rice and *New Orleans Mourning* by Julie Smith. Yet on every previous trip to New Orleans it seemed as though I had somehow landed on another planet. It was dirty, it smelled funny, and Lord, was it hot. It was like every other place to me: alien and foreign, and I was unwelcome.

But this time, the city was full of its strange magic, and I could feel it as I walked along the cracked and broken sidewalks of the French Quarter, staring up at the evening clouds stained pink by reflecting the neon of Bourbon Street back down. *You belong here*, the city seemed to be whispering to me in the dulcet tones of a practiced seductress. *Join me and all of your dreams will come true.*

And I knew, in that moment, that it was true. Tampa had never seemed like home to me; none of the cities I had lived in ever had. But there was something about this place . . . that quiet whispering inside my head that wouldn't stop. I was captured in her spell, falling deeper in love with every passing moment. And as I spent that weekend wandering the quiet streets of the Garden District, riding the streetcar, and dancing all night long in the gay bars, it kept up its steady patter.

You belong here. Join me and all of your dreams will come true. I will make you happier than you ever imagined in your wildest dreams, and I will show you how to live and enjoy your life. I will teach you how to dance.

I returned to Tampa from that glorious weekend in New Orleans with a new mission in life; I was inspired for the first time in years. My dream had always been to be a writer, and while from time to time in the previous thirty-three years I would make a stab at it, I would eventually get discouraged and give up again. But New Orleans had whispered to me of possibilities, possibilities that this time seemed real.

I started writing again—a dream I had abandoned years earlier.

Dancing in the gay bars had been so much fun. The boys in the New Orleans bars were friendlier and more welcoming than I had ever experienced before in any other city. I had always loved to dance. At my high school dances, it was out there on the gym floor that I was able to find some kind of peace and joy, dancing like a madman and losing myself in the music. I felt like I *belonged* there on the dance floor. And in New Orleans, I danced again, rediscovering the joy of total abandon, of feeling the music inside your soul and losing yourself in the freedom of the dance. In Tampa at the bars, I would stand on the sidelines and watch, terrified to join the crowd—and if I ever got up enough courage to go out there, I was self-conscious and awkward, afraid people were looking at me and laughing.

Yet in New Orleans, I felt like a part of something on the dance floor. And I somehow *knew* that it was where I needed to be.

I went back to New Orleans a few weeks later, wondering if it had simply been a magic weekend—my birthday and all. But that feeling was still there, even stronger, and that second trip only served to reinforce it.

And I started coming out of my shell.

Life was a dance, and New Orleans was now in my soul.

•

From *www.scottynola.livejournal.com*:

Long Day's Journey into Night [Aug. 29, 2005, 5:30 A.M.]

Seventeen hours in the car later, we are at a hotel in Cullman, Alabama, to sleep for about five hours before we get on the road to Paul's mom.

It took us seven hours to get out of New Orleans.

If I weren't so tired, I would have a lot of choice things to say about the stupidity of Mississippi's state officials and police; horrendously thoughtless drivers; the incredible thoughtlessness of the news media in giving 'helpful' evacuation directions: "Don't take I-10 West! Go north! The highways are clear!"

Seven hours to drive fifteen miles. I'd hate to see what they consider congestion.

I'm tired, cranky, and worried about my friends and neighbors and the people who couldn't leave.

Please pray for them. The storm might destroy our house, but that's just things. People can't be replaced.

And thank you all for your good thoughts. . . . They mean a lot.

More after I get to Illinois and safety.

•

I RETURNED TO NEW ORLEANS again for the Lazarus Ball, a huge costume party raising money for Project Lazarus, an AIDS hospice. The Lazarus Weekend is a big Halloween circuit party, really—and it was my first ever experience with such a thing. (Truth be told, I'd been so sheltered I'd never even *heard* of a circuit party.) I'd worked long and hard on my costume. I was going as an Egyptian, and drove all over Tampa looking for the proper materials, headdress and so forth. I was very excited about the weekend, mainly because I was going to get to dance again. I was losing weight and starting to feel better about myself—and I was also writing. Not every day, and the stuff I was writing might not have been particularly good, but nevertheless, every week I was actually sitting down and creating again for the first time in years. And it felt good.

The weekend was amazing. I danced every night until dawn. I met wonderful, friendly guys from all over the country—and beautiful and muscular as they were, they were nice to me. I was starting to feel like I was part of a community for the first time since I'd come out. I was no longer the outsider.

Move here and I will help make your dreams come true, New Orleans kept whispering to me all weekend long. I was happy, and that weekend I realized that the happiest moments of my life had all occurred over a period of two months—and they all occurred in New Orleans. I cried when I went to the airport to fly home. I didn't want to leave. I was making friends in New Orleans— genuinely kind people that I wanted to know better.

I wanted to keep dancing.

•

From *www.scottynola.livejournal.com*:
Land of Lincoln [Aug. 30, 2005, 9:43 P.M.]
We made it here safely.

Spent the whole day watching television and wondering if this is what the Atlanteans felt like after their island sank.

Glad to see Poppy Z. Brite posted. Was terribly worried about her. We were supposed to have lunch next week. Sigh.

Am feeling very bitter and abused by life.

I know I am one of the lucky ones. I got out. But it's hard to feel particularly lucky when you are watching television and seeing your entire life destroyed. Destroyed.

Homeless. Unemployed. Don't know if most of my friends are alive or dead. Everything I owned is gone, except some clothes, my laptop, computer disks, and the iPod.

I know that I am luckier than most. I am alive. I have shelter and food and have been drinking coffee in the morning and Pepsis for the rest of the day. I sleep in a bed at night under a ceiling fan to keep me cool. I have limited Internet access and I have a laptop computer. My family has not had to worry about me; they've known I was okay since well before K-Day. I have nothing to complain about in the face of the worst human suffering witnessed in this country since the Emancipation Proclamation.

But the coffee I drink isn't mine, nor is the bed or the television. I am sleeping under a roof I don't pay for.

I used to be very proud before K-Day. I didn't want, solicit, or welcome any kind of assistance that wasn't career-oriented. I didn't lean on people for emotional support—for that matter, support of any kind other than what I had earned. I knew I had a career I was proud of, had done work in which I took a great deal of pride, and was finally, after a long struggle, starting to reap the rewards of all of my hard work.

It never occurred to me that it could all be taken away from me in a matter of days.

My weekend had been planned. Friday night Paul and I went to a housewarming party some friends had in Mid-City New Orleans, just off of Carrollton Avenue. It was a fun party; I saw people I genuinely liked yet rarely saw. Most of the party attendees were in the Master's program at UNO for creative writing—a program I had hoped soon to be a part of. I was going to get up early on Saturday morning and work all day on rewriting a novel and editing an anthology I wanted to finish. I was almost completely caught up on my editorial work for Haworth. I was very excited about the work I was going to do, and I was in the process of formalizing a schedule for the fall in both editing and writing. I was going to take Sunday off, and I was going to try to talk Paul into joining me at Tea Dance that night. I had gotten a lot accomplished already that week and was looking forward to keeping that momentum going.

Yet Saturday morning everything changed; my carefully laid plans to be forever disrupted.

We spent Saturday watching Katrina coverage until we couldn't take it anymore, and decided to go down to the Quarter to have a few drinks. We had already decided to get up early on Sunday and see what the storm was doing; it was still plenty of time to leave. But we didn't really think we would have to, so we didn't really prepare. We prepared to ride it out on Saturday afternoon, stocking up on water and food.

Sunday morning Paul woke me up, his voice different than I have ever heard it in ten years. "Honey, I think we need to go."

I bolted out of the bed and ran downstairs, and stared in horror at the Weather Channel. It was too late for the storm to turn enough to spare the city; the damned storm was way too big. Jorge, Ivan—the others we hadn't left for were much smaller if just as deadly; and the small jog they took east before landfall was just enough. But this was different.

I don't really remember much of the rest of that morning. I remember running about the apartment as Paul packed clothes, a sense of shock and dread numbing me to everything that was going on around me. At some point a friend called, advising us he was leaving and was taking someone I was planning on getting out. We unplugged appliances, moved things, and begged our neighbors to go with us, to no avail.

"Don't forget the passports and birth certificates!" I remember shouting up the stairs at one point. I also remember this horrible feeling that we weren't moving fast enough, we had to go faster, faster, faster. . . .

We originally planned to take I-10 West and go to Houston. I was certain there were no hotel rooms there, but we would be out of harm's way. A friend was already sheltering in Lafayette and had wanted us to go there, so maybe we would do that. We weren't really sure, but finally were convinced by the news media to take I-10 East out of the city, take 12 W and take I-59 North and go to Paul's mom's.

The gas stations were closed, but I had three quarters of a tank and I figured I could get it somewhere north of the city. After all, if everyone was going west. . . .

It was a nightmare on I-10 East. The traffic crawled slowly along, and the tension continued to build as we listened to the terrorizing reports on the radio. Yet as our nerves jangled we saw amazing things on the highway. We saw church vans filled with children. We saw people pulling trailers from U-Haul and boats. I saw one seven-year-old driving a truck while his father ran along behind trying to hook up the brake lights on his boat trailer, and doing a good job. Tempers remained calmer than I expected. Every so often some asshole would drive along the shoulder, but there were no accidents, no anger, no fighting. There was a sense of tension, of a grim shared sense of purpose, in every car on the highway. There were family members and friends who were traveling together in separate cars that were sticking close so as not to get separated. Every so often I'd see an empty beer can fly out of a car window, or someone jump out, run back to the trunk and get water or sodas out of ice chests.

But that tension was there, that gnawing anxiety we weren't going to get out in time, and the fear and worry about all those people we knew that we didn't know were getting out. There was also that faint bit of hope that we were going to get lucky again, and all of this would be for nothing. Yet as we crawled along on the highway, and continued to listen to Doom Radio, there was that sense of a clock ticking and that we were losing the race. And we still had to get across the Twin Spans and Lake Pontchartrain. I was terrified, deadly terrified that we had waited too long.

I didn't breathe a sigh of relief until we got across the lake. Once there, we were still in the bull's eye of the storm. Yet I somehow felt that if we were still in the car when the storm came, somehow it was better to not be on the lake; I don't know why. Maybe it was the water, I don't know.

As we passed the time in the car, we talked about and wondered about all of the people we knew in the city. We wondered if they were getting out, if they were staying, and if they were going to be okay. As we thought of new people, it was a trip in a way down memory lane of ten years of living in New Orleans, and we were strangely happy, smiling as we remembered good times and good friends . . . but it still was a bitter kind of happy. There was a fear that there would be nothing to return to, when and if we were able to return. I thought sometimes about things I had left behind in our hurry. . . . Should we have taken more clothes? Should we have gotten more money from the ATM? What would happen if the big one truly did come this time? Would New Orleans survive? Or would it be a disaster from which it, we, and our friends would ever recover from?

We talked about friends we might not ever see again—friends who might get out but might not return. We wondered what the future would hold for us; how long we'd have to be gone; would it be possible for us to start our lives over again. All these thoughts were racing through our minds as we crawled along. And I kept watching the gas gauge creep slower and slower toward the red on the left side, kicking myself for not filling the tank the night before when there was still time.

We tried to get gas in Mississippi, but only one pump was working and there was a big line. I had to take a piss, but unlike others who'd pulled off the highway along the way to walk their dogs or to relieve themselves, I just couldn't do that myself. I drove around to the back of the station, and—my deepest apologies to the staff and owners of the station—I relieved myself outside.

We couldn't get gas there so we moved on. A few miles later, the needle now in the red, we found a station with gas and filled the tank. I don't remember how much per gallon it cost—that no longer mattered. My goal was to make it to Meridian and get a hotel room. My capacity for naiveté never ceases to amaze me. There were no rooms anywhere. It had taken us seven hours to get to Mississippi, and I was stressed, tired, and worn out. Five hours later, we found a room in Cullman, Alabama, and for five hours we slept. Before we went to sleep, though, we turned on the Weather Channel. There we were, five in the morning, and the storm was coming ashore. The live feeds from the city were horrifying, and for the first time we really realized the enormity of what was happening. I started crying. My city was dying, and somehow I felt like I'd abandoned her. I prayed before going to bed for the people in the Superdome and those who chose to ride it out, and most of all, I prayed for my city.

When we woke the news was good. "New Orleans has dodged a bullet!" the reporters all crowed. Mississippi, on the other hand, had been dealt a horrible blow.

We decided to go on and spend a few days with Paul's parents.

We didn't find out about the levees until the next day, and a piece of my heart died.

It would be months before we could return, if even then.

•

NEW YEAR'S EVE 1995 WAS the turning point in my life.

After I returned home from Halloween, I spent the next few months completely making over my life. I went to work and went home every night and wrote. I stopped watching "All My Children" and "General Hospital" and all the prime time shows. Instead, I sat down at my word processor and wrote. Even if it was just an angry diary entry about some asshole passenger at the airport who'd pissed me off, I was determined to write every day. I was determined to make myself a writer; to morph into a creative being with something to say. I would hole up in my room, light a cigarette, turn the machine on, and start typing. And every morning when I woke up, I would do my "Abs of Steel" tape and 100 push-ups. I was reinventing myself. No more out-of-shape wallflower; no more loser ticket-counter agent. I stopped eating fast food and made healthier eating choices; I gave up soda. And weight started dropping off of me. My waist was shrinking. And I was starting to feel more confident. *If I can keep this up till New Year's*, I told myself every day, *then I will join a gym*.

And always, in the back of my mind, was the thought: *And as soon as I can I will move to New Orleans.*

I stopped going out in Tampa. My reinvention took up too much of my time and was more interesting to me than the tired bars there.

My clothes no longer fit; they were all too big and hung off me.

I decided to visit my friend Lisa and ring in the New Year in

New Orleans.
  I was ready to dance.
  I was ready to start living.

•

From *www.scottynola.livejournal.com*:
We Will Be Back [Sep. 1, 2005, 11:48 A.M.]
I want to apologize to all of you who read my blog.

The other night, I posted a rather bitter entry about my
situation in the wake of Hurricane Katrina's destroying my home
city.

Paul and I were lucky; luckier than many. We had the available
cash, a working car, and thus the ability to get out before
the storm hit and get shelter. So many others were not able
to get out; so many are still trapped there at this writing,
without food, water, electricity, and working communications.
And unfortunately, the human capacity for evil has once again
shown its ugly face in the aftermath of this tragedy. Rather
than everyone working together and cooperating—as the vast
majority did and continue to do—there are those selfish, "me-
only" monsters the human race continues to produce who are making
the situation worse for everyone without caring. At this moment,
the evacuation of the people trapped in the Superdome has ceased
because of gunfire in the vicinity; the evil, thoughtless actions
of a few monsters have made the situation worse for so many
helpless others.

And my distrust and distaste for the media continues to
grow. On Tuesday, when reports of looting began to fill the
airwaves, the footage shown of the looters showed that many of
them were actually taking necessities: diapers for babies and
small children, food, and water. Yet the media did not point this
out. They merely showed the footage with commentary about how
the city is descending into lawlessness; rather than demanding

answers on why the federal government was not intervening.

And yesterday, when the major commercial airlines announced they would send in planes with supplies and would help in the evacuation effort, again, the reporters fawned over their generosity, but chose not to mention that each and every one of those airlines cancelled their flights out of New Orleans on both Saturday and Sunday, stranding thousands of tourists with no other way out. It was still safe to fly up until late Sunday evening, yet the airlines, concerned with their planes and their bottom line, cancelled flights with reckless disregard for human life. They should all be held criminally liable—isn't reckless disregard for human life a crime?

It is impossible, and almost certainly not human, to watch the footage and not feel rage. But even that rage should be tempered with understanding. I cannot help but feel compassion for the parents, trapped by their poverty, who are worried about feeding their children and getting them water. But some of my rage is directed at the media, and its criticisms, in hindsight, of Mayor Nagin and Governor Blanco. Why isn't anyone asking why President Bush ignored the coming storm situation and did nothing, leaving it to the states of Louisiana, Mississippi, and Alabama to prepare on their own without federal assistance? Oh, that's right: there isn't a Bush sibling in the statehouses of Jackson, Baton Rouge, and Montgomery—and the electoral votes of those three states (all red, I might add) aren't as important as those of Florida. And the reactions of some assholes e-mailing CNN: "The place is below sea level. It shouldn't be rebuilt, and anyone who wants to return there doesn't deserve our help."

Really?

This small-minded and incredibly stupid mentality can be extended to Californians with their earthquakes, Kansans with their tornadoes, and so forth. There is no place in this country, nay, in this world, that is completely safe from natural disaster. Yes, hurricanes are different than other natural disasters in that there is time to prepare and time to evacuate. And the thought that some smug asshole can sit at his computer in the currently safe environment of Ohio or someplace like that and pronounce judgment on his fellow human beings fills me with anger. Yeah, say that to my face, asshole—and hope that your health insurance is paid up, because when I am done with you, you are going to fucking need it.

Yet this mentality is in the minority, and again, the vast majority of Americans are stepping up to the plate with compassion and doing something, whatever they can, to help the destitute. Those people are the backbone of this country, people who understand what the American spirit is all about and also realize that the next time, it could be them.

But I have confidence. New Orleanians are a strong, stubborn, and cranky bunch. We love our city, despite its flaws, and we will rebuild it. The connection we all feel to our city runs deep, and seeing it in ruins fills all of us not with despair but a desire to roll up our sleeves and get to work as soon as it is safe to return. Our city will rise like a phoenix from the ashes of this disaster, and Paul and I will both be there to help in its rebirth.

I also want to take this moment to thank everyone for their wishes and thoughts and prayers; once again, I have been blown away by the generous mentality of my fellow humans. It is impossible to not be moved to tears by the kindness of strangers.

Some of you have asked for news of people I know: Jean Redmann is safe in Texas; Julie Smith and her husband evacuated early Sunday morning. I haven't heard from them, but I am sure they are safe and sound somewhere and will eventually resurface. Each day, the list of friends and loved ones who are safe continues to grow. Every time the phone rings, it's someone else checking in, and my eyes fill with tears of gratitude. Will I ever be all cried out?

Also, the circuit boys, so condemned by the gay community,

have also risen to the occasion. I was notified yesterday by a friend that the guys who were coming for Southern Decadence are starting a campaign to get all those who were planning on coming to donate the money they would have spent over the weekend to the Red Cross for hurricane relief.

The human capacity for love and compassion never ceases to amaze me.

We will return. We will rebuild. And we will revive that unexplainable magic that New Orleans has always had.

•

THAT NEW YEAR'S WEEKEND IN New Orleans was amazing.

It was even better than Halloween.

I met so many guys I couldn't remember them all. I didn't pay for a single drink all weekend. I was flirted with, kissed, touched, and felt up. I had more sex than I'd had the previous year— granted, it was only twice, how sad was that—but New Orleans was giving me a taste of what she had in store for me, and my love was deepening.

Her music was playing in my heart and soul.

•

From *www.scottynola.livejournal.com*:
Until We Meet Again in New Orleans [Sep. 2, 2005, 3:20 P.M.]
I am touched by the response of my readers and my friends and the kindness of strangers.

I am horrified daily by the pictures coming out of New Orleans, although today there was hope. Supplies and the military arriving— too little, too late, perhaps but better than nothing—and I am appalled by the media. Continually appalled.

Rita Crosby. Someone needs to give that bitch a brain

transplant. Talking to the Mississippi governor last night, she asked questions that only pertained to New Orleans. Gosh, don't you think he had other things on his mind? And you call yourself a journalist? Jesus fucking Christ!

New Orleans is my home, and I will return there once the water is gone and the city is safe again. But watching the images on television, I found myself in complete and utter disbelief—not only that this is happening to my city but in the United States of America. I felt like I was watching Somalia, Baghdad, Bosnia . . . not New Orleans.

This is a national disgrace, and we have the politicians—not just the bastard in the Oval Office, but all of them—to blame for this.

It is our national elected officials who have for years drained off the Southeast Louisiana Flood Project. All of them. They can point fingers at each other all they want to, but they are all to blame. The Democrats for allowing the Republicans to run roughshod over them and not standing up and telling the truth and bringing attention to our nation's problems, because it might cost them reelection. We, as a nation, liberal or conservative, have allowed this country's soul to be sold to the modern day Satan of oil. You want an axis of evil? Try Big Oil, Big Tobacco, and Big Religion—and guess what? All of them back the Antichrist who stole the 2000 election and whose evil lapdog, Karl "Jabba the Hut" Rove, made the 2004 election about sin and salvation instead of what is best for this nation.

It is time, America, to take our country back. It is time to drive these self-serving bastards out of power. All of them, starting with Bush. I want him not only impeached, I want him and his cohorts burned at the stake.

Marie Antoinette had her cake. Condoleezza "Minute" Rice has her Ferragamos. That's right. She went shoe shopping while thousands died. THAT IS HOW MUCH THIS ADMINISTRATION CARES ABOUT ITS PEOPLE.

The only silver lining I see in the current situation is that maybe, finally, America will wake up in the wake of this horror and see Bush for what he truly is. There is no compassion, no empathy, no soul in him. Just look into his eyes. The eyes are the windows to the soul, and there is nothing behind his, except evil.

Let the Fundamentalists blame the destruction on sin and gays. Let them show the world that they aren't truly Christians, so that the real Christians can see them for the false idols they truly are and reject them for false prophets whose only God is Mammon.

Where is the help from Pat Robertson? Where is the help from Jerry Falwell? Rush? Ann? Where is the compassion and humanity that Christ taught, insisted upon from his followers?

And can ANYONE really read the New Testament and believe that Jesus would have wanted this to happen? Don't you think that those poor people of color trapped there in the city without food and water GO TO CHURCH EVERY SUNDAY?

Yes, I am angry. I am sick and tired of these monsters being in power and swaying people to their side with their inhumanity. What is happening in New Orleans is the ultimate SYMBOL of this administration, exposing them once and for all to the light of day.

And never doubt, Repent America and others of your evil ilk, that the City of Sin will rise again—more beautiful and safer than ever before. And Americans will flock there, to enjoy it and revel in its atmosphere and permissiveness. We will be back, and one day I and everyone will gather at the levee at the foot of Jackson Square and raise a glass of champagne to our lovely lady who has returned from a much-needed face-lift, and toast our spirit which you will never understand in your small minds and shriveled souls . . . because it is just that; a spirit of love and compassion and beauty that you can never experience—so therefore you must hate and try to destroy it. I don't hate you.

I pity you.

As I said before, New Orleans will once again be the jewel of the South; the shining diamond in the tiara that is the United States. It is a great city, it will become a greater city.

And one last thing—blaming natural disasters on sin is really kind of stupid—explain Amsterdam, assholes. Explain Amsterdam.

And so, for now I toast everyone in this country who truly understands what this country is about; who understands what it like to be a real human being with a heart, brain and soul.

Until we meet again in New Orleans.

●

IF I THOUGHT NEW ORLEANS had shown me her face before, I was wrong.

My first Mardi Gras showed me a side of my beautiful lady I couldn't have fathomed before.

Once again I stayed with my friends Lisa and her sister Carrie. I went to parades, I danced, I caught beads and plush toys and celebrated the joy that is life in New Orleans.

And I cried when I flew out on Ash Wednesday. I cried to leave my home and return to the outside world; a place I didn't belong, a place I didn't feel welcome.

And I vowed, yet again, as the plane taxied down the runway, that I was going to make New Orleans my physical home soon.

●

From www.scottynola.livejournal.com:
The French Quarter Lives [Sep. 2, 2005, 8:21 P.M.]
While I am not a fan of Fox News—usually I refer to it as Faux News—I will always be grateful to them because today they had a camera crew in the French Quarter.

Saint Louis Cathedral still stands. Andrew Jackson still sits astride his rearing horse in the Square. The Cabildo and the Presbytere are still there, windows and shutters and roofs intact. The Desire Oyster Bar on Bourbon Street survived. The Quarter still lives.

I started crying. I couldn't help myself, and even as I type this, my eyes continue to fill with tears and there are catches in my throat. As long as the Quarter is there, New Orleans will survive. The Quarter is our heart and soul, and it means so much to so many of us.

Many people think the Quarter is tacky, a blight, an embarrassment to a modern city with its strip joints, sex clubs, and gay bars. But those are people who don't know the Quarter. It is a place of incredible beauty; of architecture so gorgeous it takes your breath away when you look at it. After ten years in New Orleans, I still marveled every time I walked its streets and cracked sidewalks. The grace and loveliness of the Ursulines convent; the magnificence of the Beauregard-Keyes mansion; the smell of grease from the Clover Grill, and the Lucky Dog vendors with their huge hot-dog-shaped carts. The Quarter is a Pimm's Cup at the Napoleon House, beignets at Café du Monde, and the bells ringing at Saint Louis Cathedral. I have written five novels about New Orleans, and at least a part of each book is set in my French Quarter, with its one-way streets, lack of parking, and bizarre street cleaning schedule.

The Quarter is a neighborhood, where everyone knows everyone and greets each other on the street with a smile as they carry their groceries home from Matassa's or the A&P on Royal Street. I've been to parties at Pat Mason's gorgeous apartment on the Square, at Marda Burton's graceful apartment on Royal Street, and at Rip and Marsha Naquin-Delain's place on Bourbon Street.

It is courtyards with elephant ferns and fountains, wrought iron lace on the balconies, and the big "UNEEDA BISCUIT" sign on the side of a brick building on Dumaine Street that always made me smile when I stood on the balcony at Café Lafitte in Exile.

I've had my fortune told in the Square. I've had drinks at

Galatoire's. I've stuffed myself with more shrimp po'boys than I care to remember. I've enjoyed every minute I have spent in my Quarter, and I thank the heavens that my Quarter is there.

The rebuilding of New Orleans is going to be a long and arduous struggle, and it won't be easy. In the wake of the flooding, the looting and the fires, there will be disease from the filth in the streets and the contaminated water. Perhaps the storm liberated bodies from the above-ground graves. There are corpses floating in our streets, bodies trapped in inaccessible houses, and the smell is going to be horrible. But the Quarter, as I have written so often, has always been fragrant with a strange mixture of bougainvillea, sweet olive, magnolia, vomit, piss, grease, and sour alcohol.

New Orleans has always been a haunted city: haunted by a long history of slavery and death, Jim Crow and poverty. Ghosts walk the streets of my city, and those ghosts are a part of its magic, it mystery, and its charm. But unlike other places, New Orleans never turned its back on its ghosts and pretended they didn't exist. We embraced them, welcomed them, and bought them a drink. We didn't pretend our history was mythological and all happy. We remember the yellow fever epidemics that killed a third of the population. We couldn't ignore slavery, because the holes in the brick walls of the slave quarters, where the manacles were, are still there. We did not forget because we never bulldozed over our heritage, unlike so many other American cities that have done so in their efforts to rewrite their histories and their pasts.

Those ghosts will be joined now by those created by Katrina: ghosts of the dead, ghosts asking questions as to why they had to die. We owe it to those who died there, who continue to die there, to rebuild the city and make it a safer, better place than it was before.

There were problems in New Orleans before Katrina. A faltering public school system, mind-numbing poverty, and crime were all a part of the mosaic that made up this strange city that always seemed somehow out of place in North America. It is now up to us to rebuild our city from the ground up—and maybe to make the city a better place for all of its citizens. Our crumbling schools will now be rebuilt, and perhaps we can get better teachers and more money into that system to finally break the horrible cycle of poverty and crime.

The housing projects, which bred drug use and crime, were a national disgrace; almost impossible to believe that Americans had to live under such conditions. It is not only an embarrassment to the city of New Orleans but also to Americans everywhere. This is the wealthiest nation on earth, and we owe it to our poor to help them break out and fulfill the AMERICAN DREAM of a better life, and an even better one for our children.

It is time to put politics aside. It is time to come together as a nation and heal the wounds of racism, sexism, and homophobia. The hate has to go. It is past the time for all of us to mature as human beings and understand that we all have to work together for the betterment of everyone.

We owe it to the ghosts walking the streets of New Orleans.

The French Quarter is the heart of New Orleans, and it is still beating. It might be a weak heartbeat, but the beat is there. The body of our city might be crippled, it might be damaged, but the heart survives.

I am trying to be a better person, to understand the root of hatred and oppression that creates monstrosities like RepentAmerica.com. I am sick of being hated for who I am. I am sick of being blamed for tragedies because I exist. I am a human being. I am an American citizen, born and raised in this country, and while sometimes I am embarrassed to be an American, I am still proud of my country and I would rather live here than anywhere else.

Let us learn from the ghosts of New Orleans. We owe our dead something. Let the lesson of Katrina be just that: to treat one another with dignity and to work together to make the future better for everyone, regardless of race, class, sex, or sexuality.

The French Quarter lives, and New Orleans will live again. But please, everyone, let's make not only our city better, but let's make our nation better for all of its citizens. Let us all learn from the ghosts of New Orleans.

They are crying out to us. Let's not ignore them any longer.

●

ONE NIGHT, I WAS WORKING on a short story and smoking when my phone rang. It was my friend Lisa from New Orleans.

"Greg, you know how I always say you remind me of a friend of mine?" she asked,

"Um, yeah." I replied.

"Well, my friend's name is Paul and he lived in Minneapolis." She went on, "He was just here, and he's going through a bad time, and he doesn't have any gay friends he feels he can talk to about everything, and I immediately thought of you. Do you mind if I give him your address and phone number?"

"No, I don't mind." I said. We talked for a few minutes longer, than we hung up and I went back to the story I was writing.

I didn't give it another thought.

A few weeks later, a package arrived for me from Minneapolis. I opened it with some wonder, having completely forgotten my phone conversation with Lisa. In it was a mix tape, a CD of Sade's greatest hits, a couple of books, and a letter. I started reading the letter. It was like nothing I'd ever received, or read, in my life. It was five pages long, and an introduction to Paul. He poured his heart in his letter, and as I read on, I began to get a little uncomfortable with this deep introspective look into the life of a complete stranger. yet at the same time, I felt as though he was talking about *my* life; I could so completely identify with the emotions and experiences he'd had.

I turned on my computer and wrote back.

•

From my diary:

It is rather hard to believe that it has only been a week since Paul and I left New Orleans and became refugees.

I've no sense of time or day anymore; this last week seems to have lasted forever yet at the same time it seems to have passed quickly. It all seems rather unreal to me now; fleeing north and the devastation that followed. I only know what day it is because my laptop tells me in the upper-right-hand corner of the screen that it's Sunday.

Today would have been the drag parade for Southern Decadence. If not for K-Day, right now I would spiking my coffee with Bailey's and getting ready to head down to the Quarter. I'd be a little tired, but looking forward to my day. Instead, I find myself in Kewanee, Illinois, unsure of my future and getting ready to do the hardest thing I've ever faced in my life.

Tuesday morning I am driving to Kentucky to stay with my parents indefinitely—there's no estimates of when it will even be possible to return home to New Orleans. Paul and I have faced hardships and difficulties many, many times in our ten years together, but ultimately, we have always had each other to cling to and survive it all. But now, with the circumstances we face, we are going to have to live apart for several months, minimum, in order to survive and be able to someday return.

I wrote, in e-mails to friends when we were safe, that what had happened to New Orleans made me feel as though a piece of my soul had died. Tuesday morning, a piece of my heart will. I know that is necessary for our future for us to be apart for a while, but that doesn't make it any easier. We've known from the very beginning that this day was going to come, but it seemed so far away that we didn't need to deal with it just yet. But Tuesday draws ever nearer and closer, and dealing with it cannot be avoided any longer.

The distraction of watching the coverage of the aftermath, horrible as it has been, has been helpful in that I haven't had to worry about selfish concerns about myself and my life and my career. Instead, I have been able to focus on my anger and my grief, and my compassion for those left behind. But now, as I start thinking about the eight-hour drive alone to Kentucky, I cannot help but wonder what the future holds for me. Will I be able to do my work? My writing has primarily always been about New Orleans. Do I write about K-Day from Scotty's perspective? How can I write about this from Scotty's point of view? I don't know . . . and selfishly I realize that I don't know if the Chanse series can continue as well. All of my plans for both series are disrupted now. How can I write about these characters and this world without acknowledging this disaster? And will I even be able to write anything at all? In the aftermath of the attack on Paul last year, I was unable to write for months, other than e-mails to people.

The overwhelming enormity of this all has still not completely sunk in. I can't even begin to wrap my mind around all of this. So many friends and acquaintances not heard from, their fates unknown.

The following: Errol and Peggy Laborde, Robin and Lou Ann Morehouse, Carol Gelderman, Kenneth Holditch, Marda Burton, Mark Richards, Johnny Messenger, my neighbors Michael and John, Harriet Campbell Young, Jack Carrel, Heidi Nagele, Darrin Harris, Debbie Allen, Priscilla Lawrence, Ann Charles, Jane Hobson, Greg Gitz, my co-workers at the CAN office, and so many, many others that I cannot even begin to list them all. My life in New Orleans was so full, so full of joy and love and laughter, and now I don't know about any of them, if I will ever be able to laugh again, if I will be able to face life without New Orleans.

•

AS WE WROTE BACK AND forth to each other, I was amazed at what a warm and funny person this stranger in Minneapolis was.

I was going to the gym obsessively, but despite the almost constant sex I was having—every time I went to a bar I never paid for a drink and I never left alone—none of those guys were interested in me as a person. I was a body, an object of desire—and I still felt empty and alone. I had gone from being nonexistent in the gay bars to being noticed, but it was almost worse this way. At least before I could blame my inability to make friends or to find a lover on my appearance—now that barrier was gone, and I was finding myself to be even lonelier than before.

Paul and I decided to meet in New Orleans in July.

•

From *www.scottynola.livejournal.com*:
A Christian Encounter [Sep. 7, 2005, 2:38 P.M.]
Yesterday, I drove from Paul's to my parents' in Kentucky for the duration of the Great Displacement.

It was a beautiful day, the sweet smell of the cornfields rushing through my window as I headed southeast. I only got lost once, and was able to quickly get off and back on the highway in the right direction, so it wasn't a big deal. It was, in a strange way, comforting to be on the highway and away from Doom-and-Disaster TV. The radio stations were primarily focusing on the relief efforts and raising money, which was a pleasant change from what I'd been watching on television. It helped me to regain some faith in my fellow Americans, after the horrors of the last few weeks.

At Danville, Illinois, I was hungry so I pulled off the highway to head into town to go to the Arby's. I pulled into the parking lot right behind another car, and I got out and ran inside to go to the bathroom. When I came back out, there was a big guy at the counter, waiting for his order. And by big, I don't mean "mountain-sized man built like Karl Rove"; I mean big-framed and muscular, like a football player. In fact, I was admiring his well-turned calves as I walked up to the counter and placed my order.

For some reason my food was ready before his, and I went and sat down. He finally got his food and sat at a table a few away from me, facing me. My heart sank when I saw that his T-shirt said University of Jesus on it, and then he bowed his head and prayed before he unwrapped his chicken sandwich. He was young, maybe in his mid-twenties, and I looked away quickly. We were the only two people in the place, and while I am not a small man, this guy was relatively big and we were in rural Illinois.

I sat there and ate my roast beef (I love me some Arby's) when he said, suddenly, "Excuse me, that's your car with the Louisiana plates, isn't it?"

"Uh huh." I nodded.

"Are you from New Orleans?"

I again nodded.

His face got really sad, and he said, "We're praying for all of you."

And, being me, I couldn't help myself. I said, "Not for me. I'm gay—it's partly my fault, right?"

And his face got angry, his jaw clenched, and I swear, I thought flames were going to shoot out of his eyes. "True Christians don't believe that, and we pray for any one of God's children who need help."

I thanked him as I blinked back tears, and carried my tray to dump the trash. As I pushed open the door to go outside again, he called out a blessing, and I thanked him again.

True Christians don't believe that.

May God go with him.

But then I believe He already does.

•

I WASN'T SURE WHAT TO expect when my cab pulled up in front of Lisa's house. Sure, we'd had some great phone conversations and exchanged some great letters, but what if the chemistry wasn't there in person? What if he took one look at me and just went, "blech"?

I was paying the cabdriver and lifting my bag out of the trunk when I noticed a man walking up the sidewalk carrying a plastic bag filled with plastic bottles of Diet Pepsis and packs of cigarettes. He was cute, oh so cute. He got a huge grin on his face. "Greg?" he asked.

I nodded.

His face split apart in the most beautiful smile I'd ever seen. "I'm Paul."

•

From *www.scottynola.livejournal.com*:
And How We Used to Laugh [Sep. 12, 2005, 11:23 P.M.]
I think the worst part of my exile is not having someone I can talk to.

Oh, I know I could talk to people on the telephone, but that's not the same thing. I never can relax on the phone, and all I can think of is the damned meter running—and even if someone is on their cell phone and has a gazillion minutes, regardless the meter is clicking off time, and the longer I talk the more I become aware of it.

I miss having people to talk to. I miss talking about writing, I miss talking about work, I miss talking about politics to people who are on the same page as me. . . . In other words, I miss Paul.

We used to talk so much. We would talk for a bit in the morning, but no matter how busy or tired we were, every night we would take at least an hour or two and talk about things, vent about petty grievances and annoyances, and get each other to laugh about them so they didn't bother us anymore.

And how we used to laugh! Oh, we would howl for hours and hours, until our sides ached and tears came out of our eyes. I've never met anyone who could make me laugh as consistently and regularly and as hard as Paul can. And I would make him laugh, too. We understand each other so completely that it's eerie. We know how each other's minds work, almost to the point where I can predict what will annoy him and what won't, and he is the same with me. I can say things to Paul—vile wretched things that should never be said out loud—that I would never dare say to anyone else, and vice versa. Oh, how we would howl with laughter; me in my reclining chair and him on the couch, the television on but being completely ignored. And always, always at some point I would say, "Oh, we are going straight to hell."

I have other friends, people in my life that are that way with me and I with them; my best friend and I used to nod knowingly at each other and say, "One of us," approvingly, when someone said something that could have come from one of our mouths. Maybe I'm wrong, but I think the people you can be so completely blunt and honest about everything and everyone with are the ones that are your truest and best friends. These are the people that are so much fun to watch bad television or movies with, because you can talk about how horrible it is. And laugh and laugh and laugh.

And it's so nice to be able to say to someone, "Okay, am I crazy, or . . ."

I love laughter. There's nothing better than laughter. Maybe it's because I am forty-four, but I think my favorite thing to do, even more than have sex, always was to just laugh until my sides ached and my eyes teared. As long as I can laugh, I can be happy, and I can survive everything and anything. As long as you can laugh, you can get through anything because laughing makes you feel good and happy.

Katrina was horrendous as well as ongoing; there has never been anything like it in this country, and so none of us were prepared for it. None of us were. We all believed something like this could never happen. Who didn't know New Orleans was below sea level and horribly vulnerable to a hurricane? But nobody really thought something like this could happen. We never do.

Part of the horror of 9/11 was we weren't prepared for it. How can you possibly prepare for something that's never happened before? We were all sleepy, relaxed because nothing like this could ever happen. I knew it could, but it hadn't happened yet, and surely it won't happen this year?

And I was extraordinarily lucky with my friends. They're all okay, but scattered to the winds. So many people had places to go, or the ability to get out. No one knows how many people got out of New Orleans before K-Day; the best they can do is estimate. Those of us who are not in the shelters are floating around out here, traveling from place to place, modern day gypsies moving from one welcome sheltering home to another, staying in touch by e-mail and the occasional cell phone call, with no fixed address, knowing that at some point we are going to have to settle down someplace, but still clinging to the hope that we'll be able to go home sooner rather than later. Some of my friends are already back at home and struggling to function in Metairie, Hammond, and Baton Rouge. I want to go back so badly, to even get that close to home; just an hour's drive so I can go and see for myself, not through the eyes of a camera or someone's writing. I want to walk into my house, rotten food odor and dank musty smell (not from floodwaters but from the heat and humidity with the house closed up tight) that means that the wood is wet and might rot, might definitely draw termites. Mildew on my clothes and in my rugs. Stale trapped air. But that sense of knowing I can put this to rights, it's not going to be easy but I can make this a home again, a refuge.

And that soon after, Paul and I will be back sitting in the living room, and laugh the way we used to.

That's what I want. I want us all to be able to go home and get our lives back. I want to be able to go have lunch with Poppy, do aerobics with Julie, have drinks with Pat, Michael, Bev and the Guvnor, go to Snug Harbor with Jean. I want to go into my office and order Thai food with Aika. I want to go outside and smoke with Jill, Tyson, Chris, and Darren. I want to drive to the post office every day, and drop Paul at the office on Mondays and Fridays on my way to Julie's. I want to go to the gym with Mark and see Michael there. I want to sit at my desktop with my cat Nicky under my computer, wave at Christina on her way to work and nod to Neal as he smokes and reads outside his front door. I want the lady gardener to tap on the window at Nicky every Wednesday afternoon. I want the UPS man to ring my buzzer instead of John and Michael's, like he always does—but I don't mind because he has nice legs. I want to put the trash out every Wednesday and Sunday night, and forget to bring the cans in for a couple of days. I want to drive down Prytania with the windows down smelling all the sweet olive, and listen to DIVA radio. I want to go to Lafitte's on Sundays and throw the napkins. I want to stand on the corner by my house and catch beads.

God damn. I knew I was lucky, but I never knew how lucky.

•

THAT NIGHT, WE WENT TO dinner at a restaurant on Bourbon Street and sat on the balcony, a cool breeze blowing from the river. July in New Orleans is always oppressively hot. I sat there, smiling, looking down at the people walking along as the evening light slowly faded. We talked about New Orleans, about life, and as is my wont, I wasn't really paying that much attention until Paul suddenly said, "What do you really want out of life?"

Without thinking I answered, "I want to be a writer."

"Then why aren't you doing it?"

I will make all of your dreams come true, New Orleans whispered inside of my head.

"I don't know." I said slowly.

He smiled at me. "You can do anything if you just decide you want to. And from reading your letters, I know you can write."

And I looked into his big brown eyes, and fell in love.

I will make your dreams come true.

I reached across the table, took his hand, and I knew I had found my dance partner for life.

•

From *www.scottynola.livejournal.com*:

Hurricane Party Hustle [Sep. 15, 2005, 10:56 P.M.]

On one of the list-serves I belong to, someone posted within two days of K-Day the following question:

"How will writers of series set in New Orleans handle this in their work?"

At the time, I was furious when I saw this. I was in, obviously, a highly emotional state and basically what I saw the question as was really: Are New Orleans writers finished?

Obviously, that wasn't what the poster meant, and as time passed, I began to see the question as a rather valid one. Do we writers of New Orleans series pretend it never happened, or do we write about it? Do we pretend it happened last year, and the city is already rebuilt? These questions began to plague me, and beset me with worry. I can't write about a future, rebuilt New Orleans because I don't know what it is going to be like. I can't write about what it was like in the city during the aftermath because I wasn't there, didn't experience it for myself. I, like everyone else, watched it on television—and let's face it, as hard as they tried, we didn't get the whole picture of what was happening there.

And that was a New Orleans I didn't want to write about; the looting, the rape and murder, the suffering and death. That is a New Orleans that can never exist again except as a painful memory, and we must do everything we can to make sure we never see that again—not just in New Orleans, but anywhere.

And ironically, the title of Scotty IV was *Hurricane Party Hustle*, and I had already sent the proposal in. It was going to be one of those miraculous massive storms that turned at the last minute and spared the city.

Obviously, there was no way in hell I was going to write that book now.

But it became an intellectual puzzle, and as I said the other day, work can be such a welcome distraction from the uncertainty of your life. So, I found myself wondering. How can I write another Scotty book? How can I handle Katrina and do the tragedy justice in what is supposed to be a light, funny mystery series?

And then I remembered the core truth of Scotty's character, which I always knew but finally put into words in *Mardi Gras Mambo*: "Life never gives you anything you can't handle; it's how you handle it that matters."

And then suddenly, it all clicked into place just how I could do it, how I could write the truth of this situation and write an honest book that will make people think and, at the same time, make them smile a little bit. And isn't that my job as a writer? To make people think a little bit and have a bit of fun and escape into another world?

As I've said before, I don't give a rat's ass what critics think of my work, what the pretentious literary queens with their martini glasses think, and whether I win awards or not. I don't. I don't see that as my job. My job is to write stories people can enjoy, create characters that people identify with and love, and most importantly, enjoy myself.

I love my characters in the Scotty series. They're the kind of people I want to know, want to spend time with, who somehow always manage to find the humor and, yes, the joy in life every day. Nothing gets them down for long. I love writing the Scotty books, and it makes me so happy that other people like them, too.

And I am sure the other writers of New Orleans series—Julie Smith, J.M. Redmann, Poppy Z. Brite, and so many others—will find a way to keep their series going with honesty and integrity, managing to capture their own distinct perspectives on our city. We all write about the city because we love it, and it shines through in all of our work, and that hasn't changed. The plaint I hear from all of my friends is: "I wanna go back home." It is home, and we love New Orleans. In fact, for almost everyone I have communicated with it hasn't been about if we go back, it's when.

And for most, it wasn't even an issue.

And that says something very powerful about the magic of New Orleans.

I don't know about anyone else, but I am looking forward to the future of New Orleans fiction. I think it's going to be even more incredible than it was before.

•

THE REST OF THE WEEKEND was amazing. I'd never met anyone I connected with on so deep a level, with whom I felt so completely relaxed almost immediately. We laughed and joked and giggled as we explored the French Quarter together. We decided he would come visit me in Tampa in September. We made plans, we made love. I just wanted to touch him all the time, listen to him talk and laugh and tease me.

And the morning I left, he bought me a rose.

I cried all the way to the airport, because I didn't want to leave. I didn't want to say goodbye.

I didn't want to get off the dance floor.

•

From *www.scottynola.livejournal.com*:
Lovely Rita, Hurricane Maid [Sep. 19, 2005, 10:46 P.M.]
I have had twenty-four hours (almost) to ponder the following

e-mail from my landlady:

> Was able to get into the City to check on the house. The carriage house came through okay, although it has lost its roof. Unfortunately, we did not fare as well in the main house.
>
> I think that a tornado came over the buildings and took off the carriage house roof and a large portion of the roof on the main house. The ceiling fell in your bedroom and part of the hall. I lost the ceiling in my bedroom and in my back library, the dining room, the office library and a part of Kathy's office. Also lost the ceiling in John and Michael's back bedroom and part of their dining room.
>
> No electricity, the heat and the humidity are taking their toll on the building. I have a lot of mildew in both the upstairs and downstairs of my section. There is some mildew starting on the walls in your bedroom and on the stairs. I took some pictures off the walls to try to protect them, but I think you need to try to get in and move items, if you can.
>
> You should not go into the apartment without wearing a respirator mask, long pants and long-sleeve shirt, and rubber gloves. Clothes that have not started to mildew can be put into plastic bags and taken immediately to the cleaners or washed. Make sure that you take some type of hand cleaner, like Purell, and clean your hands when you take your gloves off.
>
> If you have anything that says you are a business owner, you can get into the City (you are a writer whose business is located at 1517 Blank Street).
>
> I have been able to get in touch with Gus, the

roofer, and he is putting temporary roofs on the carriage house and the main house tomorrow. I am going to meet with the State Farm agent here in New Roads tomorrow to tell him the situation and find out what we do next.

I wish I didn't have to be the bearer of bad tidings. I'm afraid that it may be a couple of months before we can get the repairs done and the problems solved.

It's kind of hard to know how to respond.

Obviously, tearing at my hair and wailing like Hecuba on the walls of Troy would accomplish nothing. Neither would just sitting down and having a quiet cry.

And then there's the whole matter of luck, yet again. Had Paul and I not evacuated, we would have taken shelter on the second floor for fear of flooding. We might have been killed, or at least seriously injured, and had to deal with the four days after.

Wow.

But we've probably lost everything.

Nothing like starting over again at forty-four.

•

BEFORE PAUL CAME TO TAMPA to visit me, I returned to New Orleans for Southern Decadence.

And while it was fun, the whole time I kept thinking about him and how much I missed him. Men flirted with me, and I danced, but I was melancholy. All I could think was how much more fun this would be if he were here. . . .

New Orleans was a part of me. Paul was a part of me. And I couldn't be whole until we were all together again.

•

From *www.scottynola.livejournal.com*:
The Hermit of Hammond [Sep. 24, 2005, 8:23 P.M.]

I've been back in Louisiana now for almost five days in the sleepy, quiet north shore town of Hammond. Pat and Michael left today for their trip, and Michael's brother and his family also headed back into Algiers to their home this morning. So, the house went from a population of six to one in just under an hour, and I waved goodbye to Pat and Michael to walk back into the utter silence of the house, and I just fell my entire body relax. I haven't been really alone in a house since before K-Day, and the silence . . . it just seemed to echo around me in the emptiness of the house. And it is so oddly delicious. . . .

Bev and Butch invited me over to dinner, but I just want to be alone in the silence. It's going to take some time to get used to this new situation and be able to get some work done, but I will be here three weeks so I am fairly confident I will be able to do so. I just fed the raccoons. (There are six of them! And so cute! And please don't tell me they're vermin or mean or something; let me enjoy feeding the cuddly cute little masked bandits and don't spoil it for me.) Now I'm just relaxing a bit. This is my first post in a really long time; I've been writing posts but just not getting around to posting them. My Internet access has been pretty sketchy lately, and even today I keep getting disconnected, so those posts have found their way into a file folder I keep on my desktop called Queer and Loathing. In fact, one of them is being used extensively in the first chapter of the new Scotty book.

I hope everyone will forgive me, but I am sick of hurricanes at the moment, and I don't really want to write about them anymore. My condolences to all the victims of Rita. Believe me, I know how you feel, but at the moment I just want to move on from all of this—if that's selfish and thoughtless and cruel, so be it.

That last night in Kentucky, I decided that I was going to henceforth look at the future, and dealing with all of this, as a great adventure—an enormous challenge. And I have had any number of really interesting experiences in the wake of Katrina. It's funny, but just before Rita (hmmm, talking about hurricanes again) I was all settled and had a plan; naturally that's all out of whack again. So, I guess that's been the thing I've really had the most difficulty with: dealing with so many things that are completely out of my control. I can't control when I go home, when I can see Paul again, when I can return to work, where the hell is my mail with the checks. There's so much I have no control over—and I am fairly used to exercising the pretense of control over my life. This has pointed out to me how little control I—or anyone—has. I'm almost afraid to look forward and try to make any plans, mainly because I am tired of making plans that come to no fruition or have to be changed daily. Will I be able to do what I have planned for tomorrow? Who knows?

Anyway, yesterday we lost power around 4:30—which sent everyone in the house promptly to the liquor cabinet. The power came back on this afternoon around 2:30, just as it was starting to get really warm and uncomfortable outside on the screen porch, and I have been mostly remaining inside in the cool air, reading. Right now I'm reading *A Heartbeat Away*, a nonfiction account of the investigation that forced Spiro Agnew to resign as vice president, and something I really didn't know much about, eclipsed as it was at the time by Watergate. It's a very interesting look as well at the inherent corruption in Maryland politics—and again, interestingly enough, in one place the authors refer to the other most corrupt states as New Jersey, Illinois, and Massachusetts, with Maryland taking a rightful place alongside them, and I found myself wondering, Really? And here I thought Louisiana was the only state with political corruption. . . . And we didn't make the top four. Huh. Probably because our pols are too lazy to work real hard at anything—you have to work at being really corrupt.

Strange musings on a Saturday night. . . .

I'll probably go see Bev and Butch tomorrow. She's leaving on tour on Monday, and will be gone till next weekend.

And then it's time to get to work!

•

PAUL AND I MOVED TO New Orleans together in August of 1996.

New Orleans was a seductress, and like some seductresses, she lied a little. She lured us in with her beauty and magic; but as with everything, it seems, our magic lady had a dark side we knew nothing about. Our beautiful apartment, with its 1,200 square feet, hardwood floors, 10-foot windows and 18-foot ceilings, was in what was then a rather bad neighborhood. The beautiful park across the street was a hang out for crackheads at night. Every night, we could hear them doing their business out there, cars slowing down and idling at the curb. Sometimes we could hear people screaming at each other. We clung to each other in bed at night, listening to the sound of gunshots outside, and wondered what the hell had we done?

Where was our magic city?

That was also the year New Orleans was named "murder capital."

But even as we worried about finding jobs, running out of money, or the crack dealers and so forth, somehow I sensed that the city was testing us; testing our resolve.

Do you really love me? she seemed to be asking. *Can you love me in spite of the ugliness?*

Love is never easy, after all, and you've got to keep dancing.

•

From *www.scottynola.livejournal.com*:

Hmm. Look at all those Trees! Where's the Forest? [Sep. 28, 2005, 12:20 P.M.]

The Internet is determined to rob me of what is left of my sanity.

Dial-up sucks under the best of conditions; combine it with a laptop, AOL, and the overused phone circuits here in Hammond, and the best I can ever hope for is to get online at, on a good day, 12,000 bps. I really feel like I am communicating by talking into a Dixie cup attached to a string. Jesus Fucking Christ. To say it is driving me to drink is a vast understatement. I have had at least two drinks per night since I arrived in Hammond; and that's the minimum. Okay, it's not like I'm swigging from the Jack Daniels bottle—it's Kahlúa—but still. That's all I need, an intervention and rehab.

I also went into Mandeville yesterday as I needed to put money in the bank rather than continue to bleed my accounts dry. Here in Hammond, with all the rest of the New Orleans refugees, the locals are complaining about the developing traffic problem; to which I say, go to Mandeville if you want to see some traffic. What a nightmare. And it *was* a nightmare. My bank branch was near a Barnes & Noble, and so I went in and spent some money I didn't need to. I bought some really nice books about ancient Egypt off the sale table, as well as a copy of Herodotus, a new copy of *All the President's Men* (inspired by reading the Agnew book the other day), a copy of a classic because of a project I am considering, and a paperback by Dan Simmons, one of the best horror writers alive. I also bought a book about Andrew Jackson's presidency—for some reason I was thinking about his administration the other day (here's the train of thought: I was reading the Agnew book, and remembered that he wasn't the first American V.P. to resign, even though the authors claimed he was; that was Jackson's V.P., John C. Calhoun, and that got me thinking about Jackson and how I'd never really read much about the hero of the Battle of New Orleans . . . and now I have the book, thank you very much).

On the way back to Hammond on I-12, I kept thinking about what I'd seen in Mandeville. All the signs are pretty much down or damaged, and while the mess has been cleaned up, you can still tell that section of town was hit badly and was still scabbed over rather than healing. Everything is open on limited hours: 11:00–6:00. Everywhere you see "help wanted" signs; every store, restaurant, gas station, you name it; no one has enough employees. As I drove along I-12 listening to DIVA radio again, I thought about how cool it was that New Orleans radio was back up. And just as I was thinking that, they did one of those station-identification things and I realized it wasn't New Orleans; it was the broadcast from their sister station in Baton Rouge. And all of a sudden I couldn't help myself: I started crying uncontrollably—much to the horror of everyone in the cars all around me. I couldn't stop. . . . I just kept driving with tears running down my face, sobbing.

I have to drive into Hammond today to get Norton anti-virus software for the laptop, and I am going to try to get into New Orleans later this week to see the house and what I can do around there. I am frightened of how I am going to react, particularly after the crying jag in the car yesterday. I don't know if I am emotionally strong—or stable—enough to handle going into the city and seeing it the way it is now, and knowing it's not even as bad as it was.

I was so shook up from the crying jag when I got back, in fact, that I called a couple of friends in Houston and talked on the phone for like four hours—forgetting to feed the raccoons, and they were NOT happy with me. After the phone call, I went back to reading, and it took me out of myself and into a better place as the truly good writers can do to their readers.

The perfect comfort read . . . you can't ask for more than that.

•

IN 1998 JULIE SMITH CAME into my life.

By this time our neighborhood had "come back," the beautiful mansions around the park renovated and beautiful again. *Utne Reader* had named our neighborhood the "coolest in the country." No longer did we hear gunshots at night; the crack dealers were long gone.

I was working on my first novel when I met Julie. I had long admired her work, had devoured everything she had written, and was terrified about meeting her. What do you say to someone who is your hero? My palms were sweating, I had a stack of books for her to sign, and I was certain I was going to make a complete fool of myself.

However, Julie was charming; the epitome of grace and kindness. She invited me out for coffee a week later, and showed an interest in the novel I was writing. "Why don't you let me take a look at it?" she said, her eyes twinkling. "Maybe I could give you some tips."

And I heard New Orleans, whispering again inside of my mind, *I will make your dreams come true.*

•

From *www.scottynola.livejournal.com*:
Ah, the American Capacity for Stupidity
[Sep. 30, 2005, 11:10 A.M.]
Today, I went to *www.nola.com* to see if I-10 is open so I can get home tomorrow and survey the damage, and got sucked into the message boards, to discover the following:

An article in *Free New Mexican* (whatever the fuck that is) was published today, stating that all New Orleanians should simply be relocated to New Mexico (lots of space, lovely climate) and New Orleans should be abandoned. Someone actually then had the BALLS to post a link to it on *www.nola.com*, and when New Orleanians responded in outrage, then defended his posting of said link by saying things like, "The polar ice caps are melting and the oceans are rising"; "New Orleans is built on mud anyway and is sinking"; and the pièce de résistance: "It would be cheaper and more economical to build a port somewhere else."

The rage grew and grew and suddenly, I was back, guardian of all things New Orleans and skewerer of complete and total stupidity.

I posted:

> What a GREAT idea.
>
> Just so you know, and your children will someday know, New Orleans is where it is because it is the ONLY point on the river where the water is deep enough to accommodate deep-water ships (i.e., freighters) but safe enough for shallow-water ships (i.e., barges). So, by moving the port to somewhere else, you are suggesting we shut down and abandon the Mississippi River waterways—which extend from the Rockies to the Alleghenies. As water transport to and from New Orleans is perhaps the cheapest form of shipping, you are effectively suggesting that every agricultural and many manufacturing businesses between the two mountain ranges should just shut down. Maybe they can move to New Mexico? Oh, that's right. No water.

And then, with an evil chuckled, I added:

> And what about the Dutch? Their entire country is lower than New Orleans, so I guess they should just evacuate their country. Can they come to New Mexico too?"
>
> I probably enjoyed that a little more than I should.

It's really not fair to get into a battle of wits with the unarmed.

•

IN 1999, I SUBMITTED MY novel to Alyson Books. Four weeks later, an editor called and made an offer. I somehow managed to just say yes and hang up before having a complete nervous breakdown. I was laughing and crying and jumping around my apartment; I couldn't wait for Paul to get home so I could tell him.

I was waiting for him outside when he came up the walk. He gave me a funny look. "Are you okay?"

I started crying again. "They bought my *book*!"

He threw his arms around me and gave me a huge kiss.

My last dream had come true.

I lived in the city I loved with the man I loved doing the work I loved.

I was dancing as fast as I could.

•

From *www.scottynola.livejournal.com*:

Last Night I Dreamed I Went to New Orleans Again [Oct. 2, 2005, 9:04 A.M.]

Actually, that's not true; I slept the sleep of the righteous. But I was kind of expecting to dream of New Orleans last night, since I actually returned yesterday and went into my apartment.

The drive over was kind of somber. I was quite agitated as I got on I-12 and headed for the causeway, and going across Lake Pontchartrain was eerie in and of itself. It seemed so normal, and then as the skyline of New Orleans became clearer as I drew closer to the south shore I felt myself tearing up and my hands getting clammy with sweat. Metairie, though, is recovering. You can still see a lot of damage as you pass through on the way to I-10; debris still scattered everywhere, storefront signs destroyed, but there were signs of life there, and recovery. And I took heart from that as I got onto the ramp for I-10. As I headed into New Orleans, I found myself thinking weird thoughts—like where did the large red crawfish on top of the Semolina's near the City Park exit go? Did it blow off and wind up in one of the cemeteries, or did they take it down before the storm? As I went under Metairie Road, I could see the mud line along the walls alongside the highway, and the highway itself there is covered with a thin layer of brown. It was also weird because there was little or no traffic. New Orleanians accustomed to taking I-10 will remember there was always stop-and-go traffic between the causeway and the 610 interchange; I flew through there in ten seconds.

As I drew nearer to the city, I could see the damage to the roof of the Superdome. It looks like a gigantic hard-boiled egg partially peeled in an egg cup. I've always loved the Superdome; it was one of the sights when returning to the city that made me know I was home. Now, I looked at it and saw a symbol of misery and suffering. I know it is an important structure, and it would throw the future of the Saints and the Sugar Bowl into doubt, but as I looked at it as I went by all I could think was: Tear it down and raise a monument to the victims of Katrina there. I really couldn't stand to look at it for very long.

As the St. Charles exit approached, I saw more damage to structures down below—and for the first time ever getting off at that exit wasn't a problem with backed-up traffic. I felt a catch in my throat as I rolled down the off-ramp and to the intersection at St. Charles. Debris is everywhere in the Lower Garden District, but again, it's mostly from trees—but that was heartbreaking in and of itself. The massive old swamp oaks are still there, lining the avenue, but most of them have lost a lot of branches and look almost obscenely naked. All along the neutral ground and the sidewalks are piles and piles of branches, to the point they almost look like bushes planted to beautify the city. I turned onto my street—the same thing, piles and piles of branches everywhere—and parked in front of my house, and got my supplies out of the trunk: Lysol, Raid, rubber gloves, Purell, bottled water, and surgical masks. I unlocked the gate and stepped through just as about three black helicopters passed overhead, and then a camouflage-painted Hummer with a machine gun mounted on the front passed by, and the soldiers inside gave me a polite wave. I then picked my way through the branches and roof debris along the path to my front door. I put on the gloves, opened a water, put on my mask, and unlocked the door.

The smell was the first thing I noticed. It wasn't, as I'd feared, the smell of rotting food, but that acidic mold smell. Our new couch had a thin coating of mold. I sprayed it down with Lysol—maybe that will help, but I doubt it. The couch and reclining chair both are probably going to have to be hauled to the curb. My old Saints ball cap was lying in the middle of the floor and was also covered with mold. I removed artwork from the walls and placed it against the bookcases, just to be on the safe side, and then walked into the kitchen. I had left dirty dishes in the sink; they were covered with mold. Little gnat-like bugs were flying everywhere, so I laid down a base coat of Raid, walked to the refrigerator, opened the door, and sprayed in there as well, and then in the freezer, and shut the doors tightly. I then climbed over the piles of rubble up the stairs to get things out of the upstairs . . . sigh.

All in all, it wasn't as bad as I expected, but it was still pretty bad.

Sigh. But there's an end in sight.

•

PAUL AND I MOVED AWAY in 2000 to Washington, D.C., to take jobs. It was an incredibly difficult decision, but we both realized that the jobs would be good for both of our careers—and even though it broke our hearts to leave New Orleans, we did.

I cried for hours as we drove away. I didn't think my heart would ever heal. I could hear her whispering to me, *don't go, don't go! You belong here!*

We stayed for over a year, but the entire time I was gone I kept hearing the call of New Orleans, and I was miserable. I left the dance floor and hid from life. I didn't write. I didn't do anything except eat unhealthy and gain a lot of weight. But finally, we decided to give it all up and move back home. The homesickness was too awful to bear any longer, and I didn't care about my career anymore. Who wants a successful career when every other aspect of your life is miserable?

My heart sang as we drove out of Washington. *I'm coming home* kept running through my mind.

When I saw the first mileage sign with *"New Orleans"* on it, I started crying with almost unbearable joy. I cried again when we crossed the state line and I saw the sign reading *"Bienvenue en Louisiane."*

I was coming home, and I swore I would never leave again.

•

From my diary:
Home . . . Sort Of. 10/10/05
I drove into New Orleans today to stay for a few days and move things out of the new apartment, ironically, back into the apartment we moved out of at the end of June. So, while this isn't quite home, it sort of is, and I keep trying to fool myself into thinking that I am home. We lived in this apartment for almost two years, and while obviously the place looks a lot different then when we lived here—it's been repainted, for one thing, and the carpet upstairs has been removed—it is about as close to home as

I can get.

The city is starting to come together again, although not as fast, obviously, as any of us would like. My gym seems to be undamaged, just around the corner, but it's not open yet. I don't think the Walgreens on the corner is open. Although the Avenue Pub is—and I went and had myself a REAL New Orleans bar burger for dinner tonight, complete with steak fries. I have to say, it was probably the best goddamned hamburger I have ever eaten in my entire life. . . . I also stopped by Garden District Books to see Deb and Amy this afternoon (and no, Deb did NOT talk me into buying a bunch of books today). . . . It was almost so normal, just being able to drive up Prytania Street and walk into the bookstore and see Deb and Amy; I almost teared up yet again. There's more traffic than there was when I was here two weeks ago, but still nowhere near what it used to be like. The city is still ominously quiet. The streetcars aren't running either; I saw Metro buses driving along the Avenue.

I had to clean the carriage house before I could do anything else. The workers who'd done the painting and re-plastering and redid the roof left a mess, and so I got out the Mr. Clean and the bleach and went to town. Now everything is all shiny and sparkly. I've decided that it's probably wise to run all my dishes, glasses, etc. through the dishwasher before using them. Over in the main house, my washer isn't working but the dryer is; I have no idea what that means. I am hoping it means the washer is okay, just a circuit or something shut off. I'll have to call Harriet. It would suck really really bad to have to replace the washer—but again, we were very very lucky. It's weird; some things are damaged and ruined; and then something right next to it is perfectly fine. All the clothes in the closet and in the dresser are fine; the stuff sitting in the laundry basket is covered in mold. The towels Paul and I used the morning we left, which we hung up DAMP, are fine. Go figure.

I hope to get everything moved over the next two days and be back on the road out of here on Thursday at the latest. I'd like to be back in Kentucky on Saturday.

Oh, get this. THE CABLE IS ON IN THE MAIN HOUSE. Now, if I'd had high speed like I'd wanted before all of this, I could get online at super speed and post this.

My workout partner, Mark, is coming by after he gets off work at the bar at the Hilton where he works part time in addition to teaching grade school. I haven't seen Mark since more than a week before K-Day; it'll be nice to see him again.

Funny how big this place looks when it is empty. All I really remember of this place was how tiny it was; with hardly anything in it, it looks gigantic; cavernous. Yeah, well, Greg, wait until you start lugging shit over here and THEN see how big it looks . . . especially when you are moving the couch and that monster TV by yourself.

But it is sort of home, and in a way it is kind of nice to not have Internet access for a couple of days. It's almost like being out of touch with the entire world, which is incredibly nice. All I have to do is focus on what I have to get done, and all should be well. Of course, if it was really home I wouldn't be sleeping on an air mattress, but hey—it's better than the floor, right?

I am going to head into the Quarter tomorrow. . . . I am hoping Julie might be home. I thought she and Lee were coming back last week, but I haven't heard from her since.

Even with all the weirdness, all the differences, being here has made me sure of one thing: New Orleans, in whatever incarnation, is home for me, and always will be. I love it here, absolutely love it here. Seeing things like joggers on the streetcar line; Uptown ladies with rubber gloves, yet still perfectly coiffed, dragging bags of garbage to the street or cleaning leaves and branches out of the yard. When I arrived, had pulled up in front of my place and just gotten out of the car, there was a garbage truck slowly moving down my street picking up debris. A black gentleman of indeterminate age, missing a few of his teeth, hanging from the back of the truck, called, "You just getting back?" I nodded, and he gave me a little salute and a big grin. "Welcome home, son."

It's seeing bars with their windows boarded up but spray-painted on the plywood: BAR OPEN BIG ASS BEERS REAL CHEAP.

Or restaurants: NO FOOD BAR OPEN.

It just made me really really happy. Now I know the city will be back, and while our fears that they're going to glitz it up and turn it into some tacky Vegas-on-the-Bayou theme park with no culture and no charm may still be realized, it's not going to be easy for those People Not From Here who are looking to sweep in here like carpetbaggers and make some fast money and destroy what made our city so special to begin with. . . . Not as long as there is breath in my body.

And I know I am not alone.

As long as people can spray paint BIG ASS BEERS REAL CHEAP *on plywood there is hope.*

We will come back.

It may not be exactly the same, but now I am confident what was great will remain and what was bad will be fixed.

For the first time since K-Day, I can breathe easy, and sleep the sleep of the righteous.

I am so happy.

•

SINCE THE DAY I RETURNED from the exile in Washington, I've written hundreds of thousand of words, and 98 percent of them have something to do with New Orleans. I've watched my career flourish and grow. Life was joy again, and every morning I woke with a song in my heart and a smile on my face, because I was home. I ran out onto the dance floor with my arms up in the air, and I knew nothing could ever keep me from dancing again.

And then came the morning of August 28, 2005.

•

From *www.scottynola.livejournal.com*:
Surprise! [Oct. 14, 2005, 12:02 P.M.]
I feel relatively confident that very few of you will be surprised to know that it took less than twenty-four hours for me to decide that I was not going to leave New Orleans again.

I got up at 7:00 this morning, made a pot of coffee, and then went outside to clear away brush and roof debris off the sidewalks that run around the house. (Okay, I only got one side done, but still.) I then went into the apartment, cleaned out the refrigerator—an odious chore—and then cleaned all the ceiling debris off the staircase as well as the upstairs hallway. I also managed to finally get the door to the deck open (more on that later—guess I don't know my own strength, heh) and then cleaned out the bedroom closet. I also looted the shower curtain out of there for the carriage house. Then, I went for a walk just to check things out and discovered that my gym, right around the corner from my house, is not only undamaged and intact but reopened today for the first time since K-Day. I made an appointment for a massage on Thursday morning—I had already realized at some point that there was no way I was going to be finished and on the road to Kentucky by Thursday as originally planned—and then around noonish went for a drive Uptown—saw some more heartbreaking things, but at the same time saw more things that made me smile than tear up. The sign reading, "Looters will be date raped by Gary Coleman," I think, was my favorite.

Then, lo and behold, not only was my mail service open but, wonder of wonders: I HAD MAIL! (And wouldn't you know my government, deeming Paul and me a "legal" household when it comes to federal disaster relief but in no other instance—lawsuit, anyone?—managed to determine that I had underpaid my 2003 taxes and mailed me a bill, postmarked September 5. Now, I know it's probably automatically generated or something, but don't you think those bastards at the IRS might have recognized the heartlessness of sending something like that so soon after?) And then I went down to Tchoupitoulas Street to discover that Winn-Dixie, Sav-a-Center, and Walgreens down there are open, AS IS MY BANK! Oh, glory days!

Of course, by this time I was thinking to myself, maybe I won't leave until Monday of next week. . . . And by the time my favorite big badass Poppy called to see if I could meet her and her other half for a drink, my mind was already made up. I'M HERE TO STAY. Why drive all the way back up there, just for high speed Internet access? Please. It might take a while, but I should be able to get that going here, and until such time as I do, I have plenty of places to go check my e-mail. And don't I just maybe spend a little too much time on line in the first place, hmmmm? Time that could be better spent writing, hmmmm?

AND since returning to New Orleans, I managed to get an advance readers copy of the new Sue Grafton . . . not available to the general public for a while. Oooh, I just got all tingly.

And it was fabulous having a drink with the doc and Chef C. We went up to the Avenue Pub and we had New Orleans bar burgers (eat me, McDonald's—never again in this lifetime will your foul Quarter Pounders pass my lips) and swigged back a couple of Buds with the local characters. THIS was the kind of day I was missing when I posted back from Kentucky about the things I wanted to do. Is there anything better than a good burger and a couple of ice-cold beers on a Tuesday afternoon in a dive bar with friends? You just don't get that anywhere else . . . .

Also, for those of you trying to keep up with my bizarre readings, I have read over the past few weeks: *Blood and Money* **by Tommy Thompson**, long a favorite; *The Age of Jackson* by Arthur Schlesinger (guess what? Even in the 1830s the battle between liberals and conservatives was about rich vs. poor—and the conservatives were on the wrong side yet again, to the point of joining up with the slave owners for more power in Congress. . . . Big shock, right?); *Everglades* **and** *Tampa Burn* by Randy Wayne White, who is becoming one of my favorites; and now I am suitably prepped to dive into the Grafton. YIPPEE!!!

For those of you who have been wondering about my book collection, it survived; but I really appreciate the grassroots effort to rebuild it for me. Yeah, they're just possessions, but if I'd lost my library it would have come very close to breaking my spirit, and I thank you all for understanding that. (But if any of you can get Stephen King to sign my first editions, I would name a future trick of Scotty's after you—and if you're a female, I'll work you in somehow.)

Oh, and Jean Redmann stayed with me in Hammond a couple of nights last week on her way into and out of the city to check on her place, which is pretty much okay except for a few little things that were no big deal. We stayed up until 3:00 in the morning both nights just chatting and howling with laughter. Damn, that felt good.

My life is coming back—not quite there yet, but it's retrievable, and that's why I don't want to leave New Orleans. I need this city far more than it needs me—and that's what I think sets New Orleanians apart from people who live elsewhere—we have a need for New Orleans that no other place can ever quite satisfy.

Now, if ONLY I can find BBQ Fritos again, my life will be complete.

•

IN MY FIRST BOOK, I wrote that New Orleans "is about a block long and everyone is on a party line." In the years I have lived here, I have not revised that opinion.

New Orleans was always like a big family reunion. We are all about one degree of separation from everyone else here, and like all families, we squabble and argue and disagree and feud. But let someone Not From Here be critical, and like family, we close ranks.

I've made amazing friends since moving here, the kinds of friends I always dreamed of in the days when I stood and watched everyone else dancing. I've been to amazing dinner parties and have had a life that many would envy. New Orleans gave that to me, and I will always be grateful.

•

From *www.scottynola.livejournal.com*:
Queen of the Lower Ninth Ward [Oct. 16, 2005, 03:36 P.M.]
I spent the morning and part of the afternoon down in the Lower Ninth Ward of New Orleans, helping my workout partner Mark and his partner Johnny empty out their home.

They had 8 feet of water in their house. A tree fell onto their carport, collapsing it on top of Johnny's truck. The mess inside their house was, frankly, unimaginable and hard to describe. The pale blue carpet in the back room was a hideously smelly dark brown, and still squished when you stepped on it. Their refrigerator had been tipped over by the water, so it was lying at an angle across the kitchen—the refrigerator door had come open, spilling the food out (and the morning they evacuated Mark had hard-boiled a dozen eggs—mmm, did that smell good), but the freezer hadn't been opened since August 27. Everything inside their house was basically ruined, as was the house itself. The kitchen linoleum was peeling up, and when I stepped on it, the tiles stuck to my shoes and came up. Their leather wear looked like green velvet. The pantry door was sealed shut by mold; to get it off, we had to remove the door frame and use a crowbar, to reveal things that were so horrible it was hard to believe that at one time they'd been food items. The entire house smelled moldy, sour, and disgusting. We removed everything—all the appliances, the rugs, the furniture, and piled it all on the curb. And now the real work begins—the walls and ceilings and cabinets have to be ripped out as well as the floors, and they are planning on having the house raised an additional 6 feet on top of the three it was already raised. I am helping them with this project—of course, they are going to have all the raising and repair work contracted out, so I only get to help with the demolition work.

Mark and Johnny are currently living in a camper parked in the driveway of a couple of lesbian friends in Uptown; maybe 150 square feet in all. As we carried out the wreckage of everything they owned today, I was incredibly impressed by the stoicism both Mark and Johnny showed. "It's just things," Mark said once, as he tossed the kitchen table on top of the stack of garbage, "and we can replace it all." Then he shrugged, pulled his Darth Vader-like breathing mask back on and walked into the house for another load. At one point a Red Cross station wagon pulled up and gave us cold bottles of water and Nutri-Grain bars. One of the workers was from Uptown, one from South Carolina, and another from Tennessee. We thanked them for the work they were doing—the station wagon was loaded down with rubber gloves, surgical masks, scrubs, and other things they were giving out to people cleaning out their houses—and I again marveled at the situation. Never once, in all of my forty-four years up until August 29, did I ever imagine I would be getting supplies from the Red Cross.

It was oddly silent in the Ninth Ward; back before when I would go down to their house on the wrong side of the Industrial Canal, I would always wince at the amount of noise down there and wonder how they could stand it. It seemed like every five minutes one of those cars with the bass turned up to sonic boom levels would go by, blaring the latest gangsta rap hit, the streets were always filled with kids playing and shouting—but today I found myself missing the noise that used to annoy me so much. We didn't see many people down there, or much other signs of life other than the occasional car, Entergy truck, or sanitation vehicle. It was a beautiful day: the sun shining, the sky blue, and a nice breeze blowing. But the Lower Ninth Ward is a disaster area, and until I went down there today, I really had no idea of what a disaster area really looked like. Mark and Johnny, despite what happened to their home, were lucky; they lived close to the river so their house was higher than many. A few blocks away on the other side of St. Claude Avenue, just past Claiborne, the devastation was total—and is still sealed off by the National Guard. Driving out along St. Claude, I could look down the streets and see horrible things—houses moved to the middle of the street, for example—and everything down there was this horrendous shade of poisonous-looking brown.

Yet, despite all this, they were able to laugh and joke. They told me they were planning on dressing up for Halloween as "Miss Lower Ninth Ward," wearing dresses stained a dirty brown, with rubber boots, sashes, and snorkels. Another time, Mark mentioned that it would be kind of funny to dress up as a New Orleans refrigerator—duct-taped shut, smelling like rotten food, with plastic flies on strings dangling around your head.

Tonight, I am meeting them in the Quarter for drinks; they've offered to buy me a few drinks to thank me for my help. They have also offered to pay me for the work I am doing; which I declined. Friends help friends, after all, and since 8/29 strangers have helped strangers. The work is of course going to be hard; I am well aware of that, but it has to be done. And a little hard work never hurt anyone.

I am curious to see what it will be like out in the Quarter. They've been back longer than I have, and they said last weekend it was just as crowded as if it had been a normal weekend. Of course, the curfew has now been extended back to 2:00 A.M.; it was midnight up until yesterday—and people are still complaining about THAT. New Orleans doesn't like being told when to stop having fun; it never has, and apparently it never will.

I am so incredibly lucky to have the carriage house, and it's worth the clean-up work I am doing around here to have a roof over my head and power. I still don't have a working phone, so my Internet time is very limited, but BellSouth should have my phone back on at any moment (it was supposed to be on Friday, but for the first time in my life I am learning patience; no phone service is really nothing to complain about) and once it is, I'll be back online, posting more regularly and answering e-mails and getting back to work.

I've managed to get most of my own apartment cleaned out;

there's still about a morning's worth of work to do over there, and I am hoping to get that finished off tomorrow. Then I have some work to do around the outside of the house, and then it will all be done and I will have my days completely free to write and to read, to reflect on life and do what I always do.

But I am so happy to be home—so incredibly happy to be home. I've also realized I need to let go of my control issues; but this post is long enough and so I will talk about the new mentality I am taking towards how I live my life from now on at another time.

Adieu for now, my friends.

•

I WAS ON ABOUT MY third bottle of Bud Light and feeling pretty good, standing at my usual Sunday night spot in one of the doorways to Café Lafitte in Exile. I was talking to my friends Mark and Johnny, when the song playing changed from "Let's All Chant" to the opening strains of that hoary old classic, "It's Raining Men." I stopped in mid-sentence and instantly transformed into someone else, a smile coming over my face and raising my hands up into the air.

Without missing a beat, Johnny turned to Mark and said, "Greg is the only person I know who can go from zero to drag in five seconds."

I of course gave him my standard withering look for a second before bursting into laughter.

Sunday Tea Dance in the Quarter is like that for me. It's my favorite night to go out—even if it sometimes means being blurry and tired all day on Monday. There's just a different atmosphere prevalent on Sundays then on the previous nights of the weekend. For one thing, since everyone has to work on Monday, the evening starts earlier. (A discerning gay man would *never* be caught dead going out earlier than 11:00 on a Friday or Saturday night.) I like to head out around six on Sundays, find a place to park, and then stroll down Bourbon Street to the Fruit Loop.

And have a few beers, cruise some boys, and just relax and have a good time.

The music is always the same—it's trash disco—which makes it even more fun. And there's a sense of *tradition* about Tea Dance. They always play this hilarious video of clips from *Mommie Dearest* over a recording of "Mamma Mia" by ABBA. They show the clip of "The Night the Lights Went out in Georgia" speech from "Designing Women" (the one where Julia tells off the reigning Miss Georgia: "Just so you know, Marjorie, and your children will someday know, my sister was not just any Miss Georgia, she was THE Miss Georgia") and everyone recites it along with Dixie Carter. How can you not smile, how can you not relax, in such an environment?

And then of course there's the napkin toss. As the song "Love Is in the Air" plays, everyone grabs a handful of napkins, and on the title line of the song, everyone just lets loose with their napkins. (I always aim for the ceiling fans with mine.)

It's magic.

My first Sunday back, I went to Tea Dance again. And while it wasn't quite the same, I saw some of the same old faces I always see. And when the napkins flew, my eyes again filled with tears of joy. Maybe there were only about twenty people there as opposed to the mobs that used to crowd in the venerable old bar on the corner of Bourbon and Dumaine, but the music was the same. The old spirit was still there.

And I could hear the music in my soul again . . . and I started to dance.

•

From *www.scottynola.livejournal.com*:
The Flood Plain [Oct. 20, 2005, 7:00 P.M.]
Yesterday I managed to get all of the roof debris around the

house into bags—well, 98 percent of it, anyway. Some of it is up in the crepe myrtle trees and I can't get up there to get them down. Perhaps they'll hang up there forlornly for months, like Mardi Gras beads hanging from the swamp oaks on St. Charles all year long. This morning I dragged that all out to the curb. Everything is almost out of the main house now; some odds and ends that shouldn't take more than an afternoon to finish up, and then it's just wait for the construction workers. I am going to start pulling up the linoleum in the bathroom and the carpet from the living room next.

Yesterday when I was driving home from making groceries, I saw none other than Poppy and Chef C walking on Prytania Street, so of course I did what any New Orleanian would do: I pulled over and yelled. They are moving into an apartment in my neighborhood, which is very exciting. Once they are settled I'm bringing the Pimm's over and making us a big pitcher of Pimm's Cups to celebrate their return.

Mark called me yesterday about going to the gym, and despite being so sore I said, sure, it won't kill me to go two days in a row. On the way to the gym, we stopped and looked at an apartment in the Bywater he and Johnny are going to be renting; it was cute and spacious and homey, and I can only imagine how gigantic it must have looked to Mark after living in a camper all this time. Then, we headed down to the Lower Ninth Ward to get his dolly from the house so he could help another friend move a refrigerator, and after we retrieved the dolly (and had a laugh at the fact that someone had been rooting around in their sex toy drawer, butt plugs and anal beads exposed to the sky), Mark drove me down to Claiborne Avenue so I could see the destruction up close.

You know how when there's a wreck on the highway and you can't help but look, even though you don't want to? That's what this was like. The silence down there is absolute. No birds, no living things, other than Guardsmen making sure nobody crosses Claiborne Avenue. The dried mud is at least 3 inches thick, dried and cracked and all over everything. Houses shifted off their foundations. Mud lines right under the roof. Holes in the roofs where people either hacked their way out to hope for rescue, or rescuers hacked their way in. On every house is the spray paint from the body patrols or Animal Rescue; on some of the houses there are numbers signifying the body count. My mind in a way seemed to shut itself down. I couldn't think as I looked around—the enormity of it was simply too great for my conscious mind to wrap itself around, so I just stared at everything, my eyes round, my hand over my mouth, every so often tears filling my eyes, and I could hear myself whispering, "My God, my God, my God," over and over again. Even though I had seen it underwater on television, somehow it hadn't seemed real; sure, it was horrible, but it was nothing compared to seeing it in person. I cannot even imagine how horrible it must have been to be trapped on those rooftops without food or water, hoping the water wasn't going to keep rising.

I know people who were trapped on roofs and rescued by boat or by helicopter; they don't want to talk about it much until they have a good dose of liquor in their bodies.

The city is healing, and every day it comes back more to life, to a closer semblance of what it was. All over Uptown and the Quarter and the Marigny, businesses are reopening every day. But we can never ever forget what happened down there in the Lower Ninth ward; we can't.

And when everything was happening, and the Louisiana politicians were on television every day, I found myself wondering where our Lieutenant Governor, Mitch Landrieu, was. It just seemed odd that everyone was on TV all the time and there was no sign of him. Well, today I found out where he was. He was using his own boat to rescue people in the city those four days.

Compare that to our president.

Mitch Landrieu has my vote for whatever he wants for the rest of his life.

•

NEW ORLEANS IS OFTEN CALLED "Sodom on the bayou"—
but we are not ashamed of that designation.

We like being able to buy a drink at any time, day or night. We
like being able to buy liquor at the grocery store. We all drink—in
one of my books I said "a social drinker in New Orleans would be
in rehab anywhere else." We make jokes about our relaxed attitude
towards alcohol:

A New Orleans alcoholic is someone who will drink cheap liquor.

People Not From Here are shocked that people still have
drinks for lunch, or that wine with dinner is de rigueur. We take it
for granted here, we do not raise our eyebrows when someone has
too much to drink—and we certainly do not look down our noses
at them with disdain.

After all, every single one of us has been there—and probably
will be again.

•

From *www.scottynola.livejournal.com*:
Rainbows [Oct. 21, 2005, 7:59 A.M.]
Remember how scum-sucking, bottom-feeding faux Christians
like Pat Robertson and the people behind RepentAmerica.com
claimed that Hurricane Katrina was God's punishment for Southern
Decadence? Well, the Friday before as I was driving to Julie's
down Rampart Street, city workers were up on ladders hanging the
rainbow banners from the lamp posts like they do every year for
Decadence—and guess what?

The flags are still there! They rode out the hurricane!

Explain that, faux Christians. Your God couldn't even blow
down some rainbow flags? Maybe you should switch allegiance to a
God with some real power. Remember how in the Old Testament the
real God was always showing up the false ones? Looks to me like

your God is the false one here. . . . Better repent now while you still can, losers. Better yet, don't. I like the thought of the look on your faces when the pearly gates slam shut in front of you and you start to feel the heat from the flames at your feet. In fact, it gives no small amount of satisfaction knowing you are all going to HELL. In fact, I am smiling right now.

•

NEW ORLEANS IS NOT AN easy place to live. It never was. *The Big Easy* is not a nickname for our city that a local came up with, and no locals use it. (It actually was named that by musicians—because it was easy to find work here.) But we put up with the difficulties—the ineptness and corruption, the crime, the usual stupidity—because there simply is nowhere else for those of us who have heard the song of the siren. We cannot dance anywhere else.

•

From *www.scottynola.livejournal.com*:
Easy as Life [Oct. 25, 2005, 11:10 P.M.]
Why is it that no matter how hard I work, I never seem to make a dent in the pile or the list or whatever it is I am currently using to keep track of everything I need to do?

Sigh. Take today for instance. This morning I spent, I kid you not, three hours getting caught up on e-mail—and still am not done. My forearms were starting to hurt so I quit. (Ever since that near-miss with carpel tunnel a few years ago, when the elbows start aching, time to quit typing for a while.) So then I had to do the errands thing—forgetting the grocery list again, which means I had to obsessive-compulsively go down every aisle of the store so I don't miss anything that was on the list that I don't remember—and then the post office and the bank and the Walgreens. I was also putting together a care package for a friend who was sick recently, and when I got home I got that all boxed up and ready to go to the post office tomorrow. Then put everything away, go over to the main house, and work on the fridge some more. I think I am going to be able to save it. Once I get all the rest of the smelly muck out of the bottom of it, I think it's okay; no rotting sludge got into the works, and it seems silly to drag it to the curb if it can be saved. Then it was get the odds and ends out of the upstairs and back downstairs to pack up books to store in the laundry room (and I decided, while packing, to give my entire collection of Elizabeth Peters first-edition hardcovers to my landlady Harriet—she has salivated over them many times and all of her books were ruined, so it seems like a nice "seed" for her to start her new library with, and they are in PRISTINE condition; they look like they've never been read; although I am sure it wouldn't surprise anyone reading this that ALL of my hardcovers are in pristine, look-like-they-were-just-bought-brand-new condition.). Cleaned and cleaned and cleaned then barbecued burgers for dinner and cleaned some more. Sent some more e-mails, then talked to Paul on the phone (he's coming this weekend, YAY!) and then suddenly it's 11:00 P.M. and I haven't written a goddamned word yet again, nor did I do the tax spreadsheet, or the contributors spreadsheet for Rough Trade, nor read any of the ten manuscripts that just arrived in the mail, nor any of the four I already have, nor logged any of them in. . . . And I am so sleepy I can barely keep my eyes open. Ah, well. Maybe tomorrow I can make a dent . . . if I don't have a thousand new e-mails maybe I can finish the ones I didn't get to this morning and . . . oh, who am I kidding? I will NEVER be caught up, ever again.

Heavy heavy sigh.

And I forgot to get the coffeemaker ready, but I have go downstairs again to turn the light off anyway so I guess I can grind some beans and put the water in and set the timer. It IS so nice to have the coffee ready when I stumble bleary-eyed down the stairs in the morning, while the water warms up for me to brush my teeth in the sink. That way as soon as I finish brushing my teeth and that horrible taste is out of my mouth, the first thing I can do is take a drink of coffee, and that is always that serendipitous moment when I know I will be able to wake up and face the day after all.

I did have a lot of energy today, though. Hope that will carry over to tomorrow as well.

I think I am getting close to having one of those moments where you just become paralyzed with terror with everything that's piling up around you, and then you start to think, damn, I've wasted a lot of time, even though at the TIME I justified it as recovering from the emotional stress, but now I think maybe I should have worked rather than relaxed. . . . Ah, well, what can you do?

The lesson of Katrina is this: If you live in a area that can be hit, YOU NEED TO BE PREPARED. THE GOVERNMENT IS NOT CAPABLE OF TAKING CARE OF YOU OR RESCUING YOU, AND WHEN THEY FINALLY GET TO THE SCENE, WELL, THEY ARE STILL THE GOVERNMENT—AND THIS CROSSES ALL PARTY LINES—AND THEY ARE GOING TO FUCK IT UP AS MUCH AS THEY POSSIBLY CAN BEFORE THEY GET IT RIGHT.

I don't give a rat's ass about FEMA (Failure to Effectively Manage Anything)'s money. But here is your tax dollars at work:

My first application, three days after Katrina, was denied "because FEMA had determined there was no damage to my property and I could move back in immediately"—even though at that time FEMA apparently couldn't get into New Orleans, and Michael Chertoff had just discovered there was a "problem" at the Superdome. (Mr. Presiduh-nt had yet to tell Brownie he was "doin' a heckuva job" yet, though.)

My second application was denied "because there is only one head of household, and we've already paid a claim to the head of your household."

Third strike: I was yet again informed, by letter, that my house did not sustain any noticeable damage and there is no reason why I can't reside in my house. This letter also stated that within ten days of my application, I would get a call from a FEMA inspector who would make an appointment to see the property with me to determine my eligibility. My application was dated 9/15. I received this letter this week.

Paul and I were not, by any means, properly prepared. We didn't empty our refrigerator, we didn't take enough clothing with us, we didn't do this, we didn't do that. But we have already come up with our plan for next time—and there will be a next time, and we will be ready.

•

MARDI GRAS 2006 HAS COME and gone, and once again the city of New Orleans lies in ruins. Piles of trash are everywhere, beads hang from trees and power lines along the parade route, and traffic has returned to a semblance of normalcy. In the period between August 29 and February 28, there was a lot of talk as to whether we should have Mardi Gras. Many People Not From Here felt that it was wrong for New Orleans to celebrate in the wake of the devastation left by Hurricane Katrina and the flood that followed. At first, this criticism made me angry. How dare people who do not live here, have never lived here, tell us what we can or cannot do? Mardi Gras is New Orleans, New Orleans is Mardi Gras. Yet now that the season has passed, I feel nothing but pity for those who voiced their opposition. Because they do not understand New Orleans, they do not understand Mardi Gras, they do not understand us. They never will, which is all the more reason to pity them.

New Orleans is not about geography. New Orleans is a state of mind. The rest of the country has a lot to learn from we who live here. We work to live, not live to work. We enjoy life, take each day as it comes, and we don't stress about things we cannot control. We squeeze every ounce of pleasure that we can out of life, because life is too short to sweat the small stuff. We understand that life is about living. We don't mourn death; we celebrate the life.

New Orleans has always been about survival, and this past Mardi Gras was a celebration of that very fact. *We survived, we are still here, and we are going to rebuild.*

Once you hear the song of the siren, and let her into your soul, there is nowhere else.

No, we haven't stopped dancing yet. And God willing, we never will.

hurricane names

martin pousson

Jungle Bunny
Pickaninny
Jigaboo

Spade
Porch Monkey
Nigger

These are the names I remember
names for black people
in the South

As with hurricanes
from the Gulf,
I remember the names,

remember where
the winds twisted, where
the tails slapped down

in the furious storms
which spun from the center
to clean everything in their path.

Mama started in the center, too
then worked her sponge
in tight circles, cleaning the house

with unstoppable force
and a powerful liquid
she called Hurricane in a Bottle.

She put bleach in the clothes,
the dishes, the toilets,
on the tile floors and baseboards.

Her declaration, even to herself,
was always the same:
Can't get things white enough.

Don't come home with no nigger
or you got no home.
Mama doesn't remember saying it

but she must have,
it's all I heard the first time
I laid under a black man.

He raised a storm
darker than dirt,
darker than blood when it dries.

I couldn't get clean enough,
couldn't halt the roaring in my ears
the hurricane of names.

contributor biographies

toni amato has been a teacher, editor, and writing coach since 1992, conducting workshops in creative writing, publication, and performance, as well as facilitating peer critique groups. Toni has had fiction published in several anthologies, including *Best Lesbian Erotica 1998–2001*, and has performed extensively in Boston and New York, as well as at Temple, Goddard, and Brandeis universities. Toni was a recipient of the 2000 LEF Fellowship and the 2001 Diana Korzenik Fellowship to the Writers' Room of Boston. Most recently, he served as editor for the anthology *Pinned Down by Pronouns* published by Conviction Books Press.

steve berman is an active member of the Science Fiction Writers of America and the author of over sixty published short stories, as well as the collection *Trysts*. His first novel, *Vintage*, as well as his anthology *So Fey* will be published by the Haworth Press this fall.

pastor dexter brecht is a clergyperson ordained by the Universal Fellowship of Metropolitan Community Churches. New Orleans has been his home since 1994 when he was called there to pastor MCC of Greater New Orleans. He holds a B.A. from Mount Mercy College and an M.A. from the University of Iowa, and has done additional study at United Theological.

poppy z. brite is the author of eight novels, three short story collections, and much miscellanea. Her most recent work includes a series of novels set in the New Orleans restaurant scene: thus far, *Liquor*, *Prime*, and *Soul Kitchen*. She is at work on another book in the series. Poppy Z. Brite lives in New Orleans with her husband Chris, a chef.

victoria a. brownworth is an award-winning writer, journalist, and editor and a longtime community activist. Her anthology *Coming Out of Cancer* received the prestigious Editor's Choice Award from the Lambda Literary Foundation. She currently lives in Philadelphia, and publishes a syndicated column titled "The Lavender Tube" about queer representation on television.

amie m. evans is a widely published creative nonfiction and literary erotica writer, experienced workshop provider, and a retired burlesque and high-femme drag performer. Her short stories and essays have appeared most recently in *Ultimate Lesbian Erotica 2006*, *Show and Tell*, *Call of the Dark*, *Rode Hard and Put Away Wet*, and *Best of the Best of Lesbian Erotica*. Evans is on the board of directors for the Saints and Sinners GLBT literary festival. She graduated from the University of Pittsburgh with a B.A. in literature and is currently working on her MLA at Harvard. She is currently co-editing an anthology on drag kings for Suspect Thoughts Press with Rakelle Valencia.

jewelle gomez, writer and activist, is the author of seven books, including her novel, *The Gilda Stories*, which was the winner of two Lambda Literary Awards (fiction and science fiction) and over the past thirteen years has become a cult favorite. She has been on the funding board of GLAAD and the Astraea Lesbian Foundation. Visit her at www.jewellegomez.com.

greg herren is a longtime New Orleans resident and author of five novels set in New Orleans, including *Murder in the Rue St. Ann* and *Mardi Gras Mambo*. He has also edited the anthologies *Shadows of the Night* and *Upon a Midnight Clear*. You can read his ramblings about life, writing, and the world in general at *www. scottynola.livejournal.com.*

dr. kenneth holditch is a professor emeritus at the University of New Orleans. An expert on both the city of New Orleans and on Tennessee Williams and his plays, he is the co-editor of *Tennessee Williams: Plays, 1957–1980*, and *Tennessee Williams: Plays, 1937–1955*, as well as being co-author of *Tennessee Williams and the South*, *In Old New Orleans* and *Galatoire's: Biography of a Bistro*. He has written dozens of essays about Southern authors, especially those associated with New Orleans.

martin hyatt was born just outside of New Orleans. He later attended Goddard College and the New School. He is the recipient of an Edward F. Albee Writing Fellowship and the New School Chapbook Award for fiction. His stories have been published in such places as *Sandbox* and *Blithe House Quarterly*. His first novel, *A Scarecrow's Bible*, is to be published in March 2006 by Suspect Thoughts Press. He has taught writing at such places at Hofstra and Yeshiva universities, the New School, and St. Francis College.

karissa kary lives and writes in the French Quarter of New Orleans and is the associate director of the Tennessee Williams/ New Orleans Literary Festival. She also helps organize Saints and Sinners Literary Festival, a LGBT Literary Festival that takes place in the French Quarter in the spring.

dr. jon lohman is the director of the Virginia Folklife Program, at the Virginia Foundation for the Humanities. He holds a Ph.D. in folklore and folklife from the University of Pennsylvania, where he specialized in Carnival and other forms of public festivity.

kay murphy is the author of two collections of poetry, *The Autopsy* and *Belief Blues* and co-editor of *Women Poets Workshop into Print*. Her poetry, fiction, and reviews have appeared in such journals as the *American Book Review*, *Ascent*, *Chelsea*, *Fiction International*, *North American Review*, *College English*, and *Poetry*. She is an associate professor of English at the University of New Orleans and poetry editor of *Bayou*. In 2001 she received the university-wide Alumnae Excellence in Teaching Award and in 2002 she received an individual writer's grant from the Louisiana Endowment for the Arts.

martin pousson was born and raised in the bayouland of Louisiana. His first novel, *No Place, Louisiana*, was a finalist for the John Gardner Award in Fiction and has been translated into French. *Sugar*, his first collection of poetry, was a finalist for the Lambda Literary Award. He has taught in the writing program at Columbia University in New York and at 826 Valencia in San Francisco. He now teaches at Loyola University in New Orleans, where he lives.

j. m. redmann has published four novels, all featuring New Orleans private detective Michele "Micky" Knight. The most recent of these, *Lost Daughters*, was published by W.W. Norton. Her third book, *The Intersection of Law and Desire* won a Lambda Literary Award, was an Editor's Choice selection of the *San Francisco Chronicle*, and was featured on National Public Radio. *Lost Daughters* and *Deaths of Jocasta* were also nominated for Lambda Literary Awards. Her books have been translated into German, Dutch, Spanish, and Norwegian. Ms. Redmann lives, works and frolics in the city in a swamp, New Orleans. Her day job is director of prevention for NO/AIDS Task Force.

Since 1996 **brian sands** has written for *Ambush Magazine*, the largest GLBT publication in the Gulf South, assuming the position of co-editor of theater in October 2002. He has appeared in the *New York Times*, *New York Magazine* and *Pride .01*. Prior to moving to New Orleans from New York, he was theater editor of the *West Side Spirit*, a publication he continues to write for. As a playwright, Sands has had works produced by the Artists Cooperative Theater and DramaRama; his play MORE was featured at DramaRama 2005, held at the Contemporary Arts Center in New Orleans. He has been a member of the Dramatists Guild for over twenty years and is a graduate of Harvard University. He has served on the boards of the Harvard Gay & Lesbian Caucus, the Lesbian & Gay Community Center of New Orleans, and Halloween's in New Orleans, and was thrilled to return to New Orleans post-Katrina.

melinda shelton is a longtime community activist, writer, and photographer. She is a faculty member in the Southeastern Louisiana University Department of English.

timothy state grew up in the Pacific Northwest, attending college in the Midwest at Lake Forest College, and completing a ten-year tour in the capital of the South, Atlanta. He no longer knows how to pronounce anything. In 2004, Timothy was recognized as one of Georgia's "Newest and Most Promising Writers" by the O, Georgia! Writers Foundation. His blog, "Balancing Boyfriends" (*www.balancingboyfriends.com*) has been highlighted by *The Bottom Line Magazine* as a "Best Gay Blog," and by HomoMojo.com's "Best of Gay Blogging." His video work has been featured in Image Film and Video's "Shorts Slam!" and his *Postcards from Graceland*—perspectives from a road trip to the twentieth-anniversary commemoration of Elvis Presley's passing— has been adapted for the stage by an Atlanta theater company.

patricia nell warren is a longtime writer, poet, and activist. Her novel *The Front Runner* was a *New York Times* best-seller, and is one of the most beloved gay novels of all time. She currently lives in Los Angeles.

paul j. willis is the editor of *Sex Buddies: Erotic Stories about Sex without Strings*, *View to a Thrill*, and co-editor with Ron Jackson for the anthology *Kink: Tales of the Sexual Adventurer*. Willis also co-edited the anthology *Bad Boys* with M. Christian and has a new anthology, *Dangerous Liaisons*, due out in spring 2007. He currently works as the executive director for the Tennessee Williams/New Orleans Literary Festival, and is the festival organizer for the Saints and Sinners Literary Festival. He can be reached at pjwillisnola@ aol.com.